The Beauty of
Jewellery

The Beauty of *Jewellery*

by Joan Frank

Produced by
Ted Smart & David Gibbon

Photography by Neil Sutherland
Research by Hanni Edmonds

First published in Great Britain 1979 by Colour Library International Ltd.
© Colour Library International Ltd. 1979
Printed and bound by Rieusset, Barcelona, Spain.
Published by Crescent Books, a division of Crown Publishers Inc.
All rights reserved.
Library of Congress Catalogue Card No. 78-59736

CRESCENT

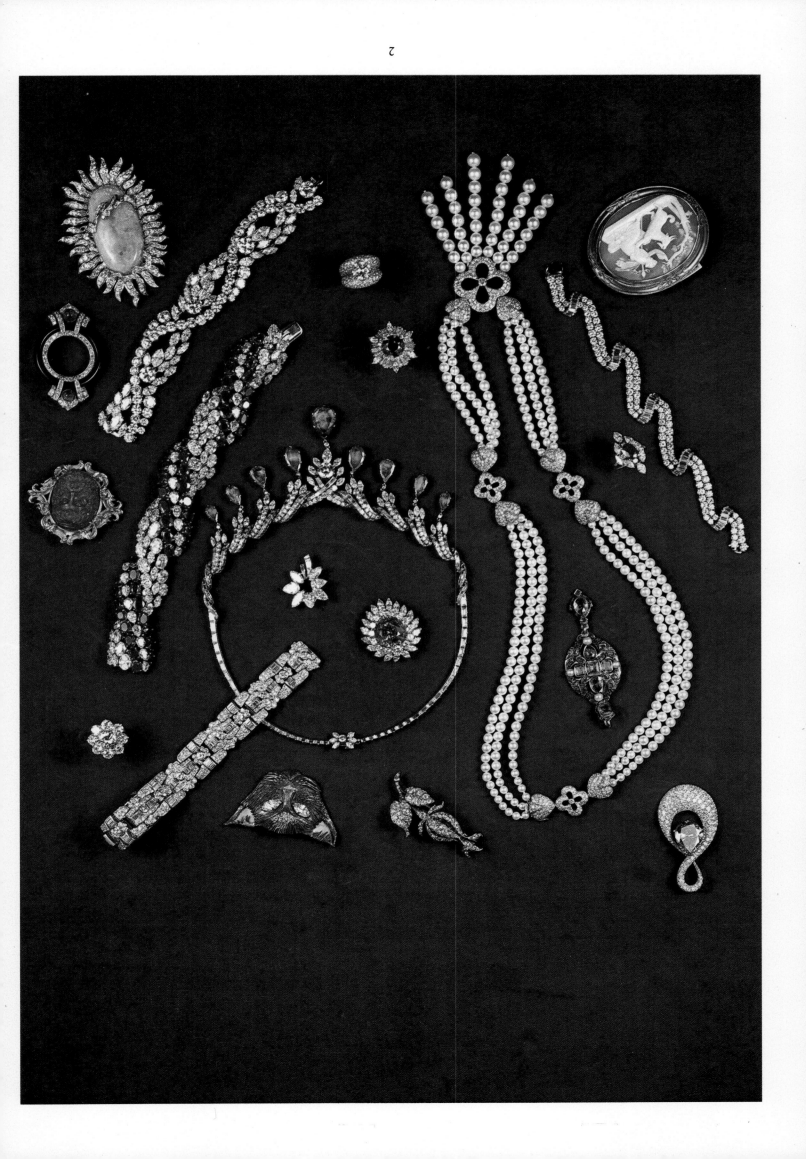

Contents

Left: *An Italian gold and mosaic brooch pendant decorated with a pair of doves on a blue floral panel with stylised borders, three drops — 3¼" long. Circa 1830. (Asprey & Co. Ltd.)*

Frontispiece: *Cabochon sapphire and diamond necklace. (Jewellery by Graff)*

Opposite: *Selection of jewellery from Garrard The Crown Jewellers.*

Introduction

Jewellery as a subject has many facets. It can be dealt with in a strictly factual way, stressing the gemmological and historical aspects or looked at in an uncomplicated manner, more suited to the possible origin of its name. The word jewellery is still undefined but it is thought to come from the French word joie, meaning joy, or jeu, meaning game. So this book seeks to court the lighter side and emphasise the beauty of jewellery and the lasting pleasure it can give the owner, however humble that item may be.

Jewellery is made up of gemstones and precious

Above: *Cut diamond. (De-Beers)*

Below: *Yellow gold, cultured pearl brilliant and briolette diamond pendant. (Garrard The Crown Jewellers)*

Above: *Rings of pink and blue sapphires and emeralds surrounded by diamonds. (Jewellery by Graff)*

Facing Page: *Navette emerald, navette sapphire, carved rubies and diamond necklace with matching earrings. Butterfly: yellow gold butterfly tremblant brooch, pear shaped emerald baton ruby and diamond wings. Pear shaped sapphire body. (Cartier, London)*

metals; part of the earth's treasure, they have taken millions of years combined with the interplay of the elements to produce. Where gemstones are concerned each one is entirely different. Never duplicated, they form an individual work of art for the owner. Gemstones are an absorbing study and it may be well to point out a serious misnomer which has crept into common usage. That is referring to gemstones as semi-precious. As well as the five precious or principal gems, comprising diamonds, sapphires, rubies, emeralds and pearls, there are hosts of others, all of them precious because they are not fabricated. Sometimes they are called lesser gemstones but it is imperative to realise that any natural gem is wholly precious and the semi part must be disregarded. It is just as wrong to say that someone is half-dead!

Owning jewellery gives a feeling of security and continuity. It is the one commodity that has a built-in value so that it can be handed on to make a bridge between one generation and another. Sometimes the design of a certain piece of jewellery does not please the recipient. In that case the item can be re-styled, thus preserving the continuity of the component parts. This re-cycling can provide a more suitable or up-to-date design for the new owner.

Jewellery expresses the personality of the wearer probably more than any other adornment. When choosing a piece it is advisable to 'fall in love' with it, because a treasured possession should have lasting appeal to match its durability; always remembering that jewellery must be treated with a certain respect as befits its precious quality.

Jewellery was originally worn by the leisured and the rich. Today the picture has utterly changed. Jewellery is for everybody and so is subject to the stresses and strains of modern living. There is no need to feel fearful about wearing jewellery: average care is all that is necessary.

The magic and mystery of jewellery is age-old. Based on legend and superstition, it is the one possession that preserves a fascinating mystique. It must be noted that

Below: *Drop Peridot ring with marquise and brilliant cut diamond top, mounted in 18 ct. yellow gold. (Garrard The Crown Jewellers)*

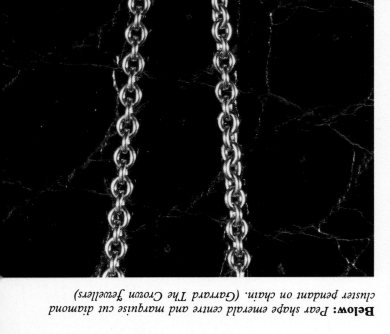

Below: *Pear shape emerald centre and marquise cut diamond cluster pendant on chain. (Garrard The Crown Jewellers)*

for every unattractive superstition, there is usually a pleasant one. This can be seen in a subsequent chapter.

One aspect that needs stressing is the versatility of jewellery, where enjoyment is concerned. There is a unique two-way pleasure about it, shared by the beholder, as well as the wearer. A piece of jewellery calls forth admiring remarks more than any other adornment. This, surely, adds to pride of possession and intensifies its attraction. As jewellery has a lasting beauty it sustains the visual appeal which never seems to flag.

When there is a developing interest in the subject of jewellery many spin-offs emerge. They include history and gemmology as well as fashion and the origin of words. This last angle is completely absorbing. In-depth study of names clarifies so much and gives extra meaning to a familiar term.

Diamond is said to come from the Greek word, *adamas*, meaning unconquerable. As this gem is most popular for engagement rings and love is meant to be unconquerable, what better origin can there be? Peridot, the lovely olive green stone has a somewhat baffling name but is supposed to come from the Arabic, *faridat*, meaning precious stone: this would of course, make more sense.

The origin of the word Pearl has not really been traced. It could come simply from the French, *perle*, or from the Latin, *perla*, or *pilula* meaning globule. Pliny has mentioned another Latin derivation, the word *perna* which describes a leg-of-mutton shaped shell-fish. A more obvious derivation is for Ruby. This comes from the Latin *ruber*, meaning, simply, red. Emerald takes rather more explanation. Its possible derivation stems from the Persian word for green: *zummurrud*. It later appeared in Greek form as *smaragdus* and subsequently was altered to *esmeraude, émeraude* and *esmeralde*. Finally, some time during the sixteenth century, it came to be known by its present name.

The Opal has a pleasingly simple origin and comes from the Sanskrit for stone or jewel. But Sapphire has a longer list. There is the Arabic, *safir*, possibly meaning blue. Then there is the Greek word *sappheiros*, which

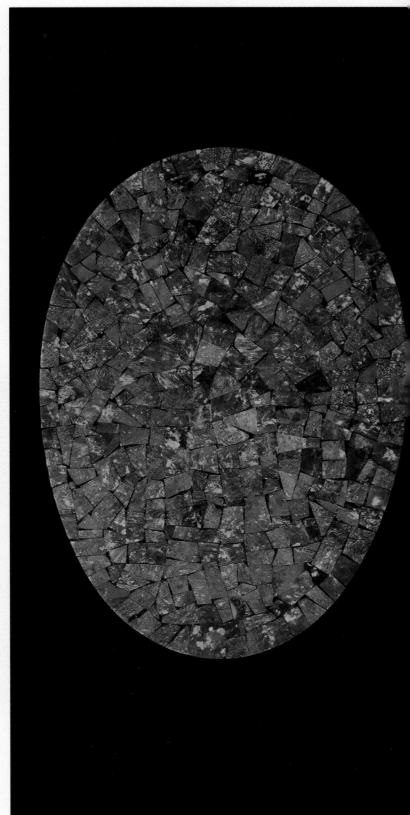

Above: *Emerald ring with brilliant, navette and baguette diamond surround.*
Cabochon ruby half hoop ring with diamond sides.
Yellow sapphire ring with brilliant diamond surround.
(Collingwood of Conduit Street Limited)

Right: *Opal mosaics on onyx backing. (E.A. Thomson (Gems) Ltd.)*

Facing page: *An important pair of hessonite garnet and gold drop earrings. Spanish 18th century. (Cameo Corner Ltd.)*

Below Right: *A Victorian amethyst and split pearl cluster brooch circa 1870. (Bonhams Auctioneers)*

Right: *Mid-Victorian cabochon amethyst, half pearl and gold fringed brooch, English. (Cameo Corner Ltd.)*

Below: *A garnet and gold brooch with a central delicately enamelled plaque of a child. French 19th century. (Cameo Corner Ltd.)*

stems from the Sappherine Island in the Arabian Sea where sapphires were found in the time of the Ancient Greeks. Lastly there is the Latin, *sapphirus*, closely resembling the name it is known by today. Garnet, could come from two Latin words, either *granum*, meaning grain or *granatus*, a seed. Aquamarine, that sea-green or sea-blue gem, is aptly derived from the Latin *aqua* meaning water and *mare* meaning sea.

The derivation of the word Amethyst is bound up with its mythological origin. It comes from the Greek *amethystos*. It is said that Bacchus, god of wine, was offended by Diana, goddess of the hunt. In revenge he vowed that the first person to cross his path would be eaten by a tiger. Unfortunately, a nymph much loved by Bacchus, on her way to worship Diana was the one to be attacked. In absolute terror she appealed to Diana to save her and, watched by Bacchus, she was turned into a sparkling white statue. As a gesture of repentance he, in turn, poured grape wine over it so that the stone assumed its beautiful amethyst colour.

The word turquoise has a connection with Iran. This

country is the oldest source of these gemstones, where it was called *piruseh*, meaning joy. When the Turkish merchants first introduced it into Europe they referred to it as, *turchesa*, the 'Turkish stone'. The French version, *pierre turquoise* also means 'stone of Turkey' and is the term used today.

The Zircon is probably best known when colourless but it also comes in yellow, red, orange and shades of green and a sky-blue. Because of the variety of colour its word origin can be more easily understood. Although uncertain it is thought to be adapted from the French *zircone*. It may have come from the Arabic *zargoon* meaning vermilion or even from the Persian word *zargus* which means gold-coloured. The Tourmaline also covers a wide range of colours, more, in fact, than the majority of gemstones. Therefore the origin of its name, *toramalli*, from the Sinhalese is particularly apt, for it means 'coloured stone'. The derivation of the

Left: Turquoise brilliant cut diamond and yellow gold abstract brooch. (*Garrard The Crown Jewellers*)

Below: A fine roman mosaic and gold set suite, consisting of a necklace, pendant, brooch and earrings, all mounted in gold cannetille work set with turquoise and pearls. Italian, early 19th century. (*Cameo Corner Ltd.*)

name Spinel, is somewhat obscure. It is thought to originate from the Latin *spina* meaning thorn or from the Greek word meaning a spark, because of its fiery colour.

Finally, when a gem is in the shape of a dome, without facets, it is known as, en cabochon. This comes from the French and means, literally, bald pate: a most picturesque term. It can be seen, from an interest point-of-view, that the origin of words, applied to jewellery, gives yet another dimension to the subject and inspires further study, as there are so many more gemstones to explore in this way.

How many people give their jewellery the care it merits as a treasured possession? The answer is, unfortunately, very few and yet it is so easy to achieve a sparkling effect with a minimum of effort. Guide lines suggest home-cleaning every three weeks or so, with a professional clean by a jeweller at least once a year. Cost depends on time taken, as is usual. If it is a simple, straightforward clean, the charge will be relatively low: possibly cheaper, by comparison, than similar services for clothes and hair.

There are many conflicting ideas about cleaning jewellery at home. The following is a safe method and

Above: *Cabochon rubies and diamond set in yellow gold. (Jewellery by Graff)*

Above: *Faceted pear shaped rubies, one navette ruby in centre cluster, yellow gold mount. (Cartier, London)*

produces excellent results. Use a liquid detergent rather than a soap-based one as the latter tends to leave a greasy deposit or film. The principal reason for cleaning jewellery every three weeks or so is to remove the film that builds up behind a setting, to which dust and dirt adhere, dulling the surface.

Make a mild lather in tepid to hot water, in a small bowl, and with a child's soft toothbrush gently clean behind the setting. Give about three rinses in clear water, to completely disperse the lather. Place the item on a piece of tissue to drain dry, then polish with a soft cloth.

Where diamonds are concerned and only diamonds, add a tablespoon of household ammonia to the lather. Swish the diamonds around in the suds and clean them briskly with an eyebrow brush. Rinse in luke-warm water and finally dip in surgical spirit to emphasise the brilliance and drain on blotting paper or tissue. Finally, polish with a soft cloth.

Certain gemstones should never be immersed in liquid, because of their particular structure. They are the opal, turquoise and pearl. Just apply a cloth dipped in the lather and then wipe in the same way, with several applications of clear water.

The best way to preserve jewellery is to keep it in a jewel case or roll. The pieces must be kept apart so that they do not scratch each other. The surface of a pearl is very vulnerable and reacts badly to hair lacquer and perfume. Indeed all jewellery should be removed while at the hairdressers to prevent contact with chemicals or lacquers. When dressing, jewellery should be put on

11

last thing.

Jewellery should be kept out of the kitchen and bathroom. Steam and grease dull precious metals and gemstones and can cause a residue of dirt and dust to form. Handbags are also forbidden territory. Particles of face powder, tobacco and dust tend to erode delicate surfaces.

The result which comes from caring regularly for jewellery can add to its enjoyment.

Above: *Cabochon sapphire and diamond necklace with matching earrings, bracelet and ring. (Jewellery by Graff)*

1. The Unfading Colours of Jewellery

Of all the beauties found in nature, colour has the most striking and memorable appeal. There is nothing more satisfying to the eye than the intense blue of a cloudless sky, or the fresh green of grass after rain. Jewellery colours have the same impact, but they offer an added delight because their colours last forever.

There is an infinite variety in natural colours, caused mainly by the delicate nuance between one shade and

Below: *Uncut coloured diamonds: picture from De-Beers.*

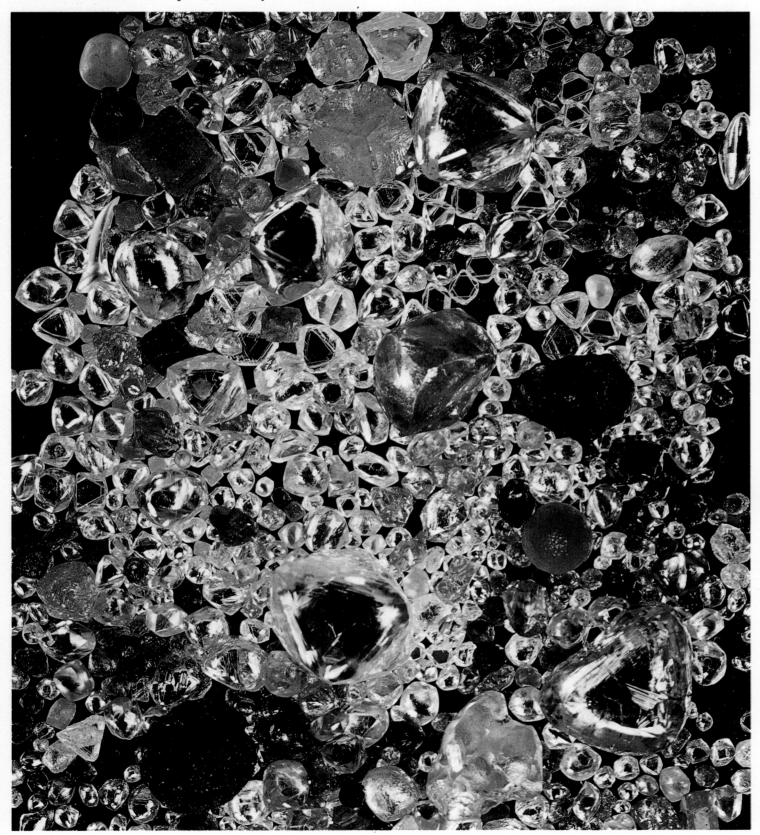

another. The rainbow is really only a sample of the whole range. A parallel may be found in gemstones. The known colours of familiar jewels have become part of the language and are, therefore, more easily brought to mind: emerald-green, ruby-red, pearly-white, sapphire-blue and even diamond-bright. Gems are usually remembered by one particular shade; they do, however, appear in other colours, perhaps less familiar and rarer in occurrence, but none-the-less fascinating.

Diamonds are known and prized for their radiant quality and usually are thought of in varying shades of white. They can come in natural, fancy colours to include sweet pea shades of pink and blue, as well as in yellow and amber. The characteristic brilliance of these gems adds an extra dimension to their appearance.

Below: *Marquise-diamond brilliant cut and baguette diamond bracelet. (Philip Antrobus Ltd.)*

Below Right: *Rare pink diamond, emerald cut. 10 carat.* (*Jewellery by Graff*)

Below left: *Rare blue diamond, pearshape. 5.10 carat.* (*Jewellery by Graff*)

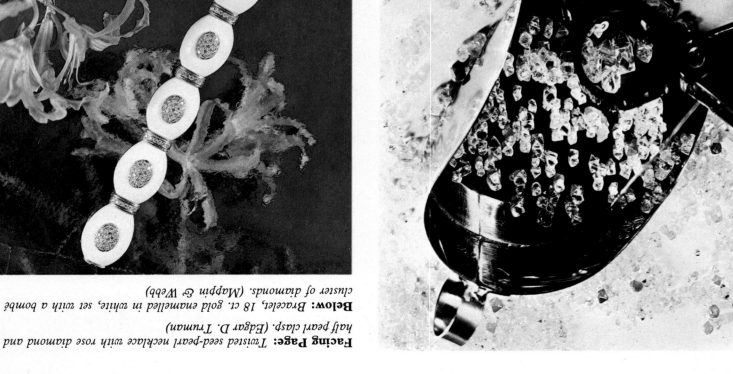

Above: *Uncut coloured diamonds: picture from De-Beers.*

Below: *Bracelet, 18 ct. gold enamelled in white, set with a bombé cluster of diamonds. (Mappin & Webb)*

Facing Page: *Twisted seed-pearl necklace with rose diamond and half pearl clasp. (Edgar D. Truman)*

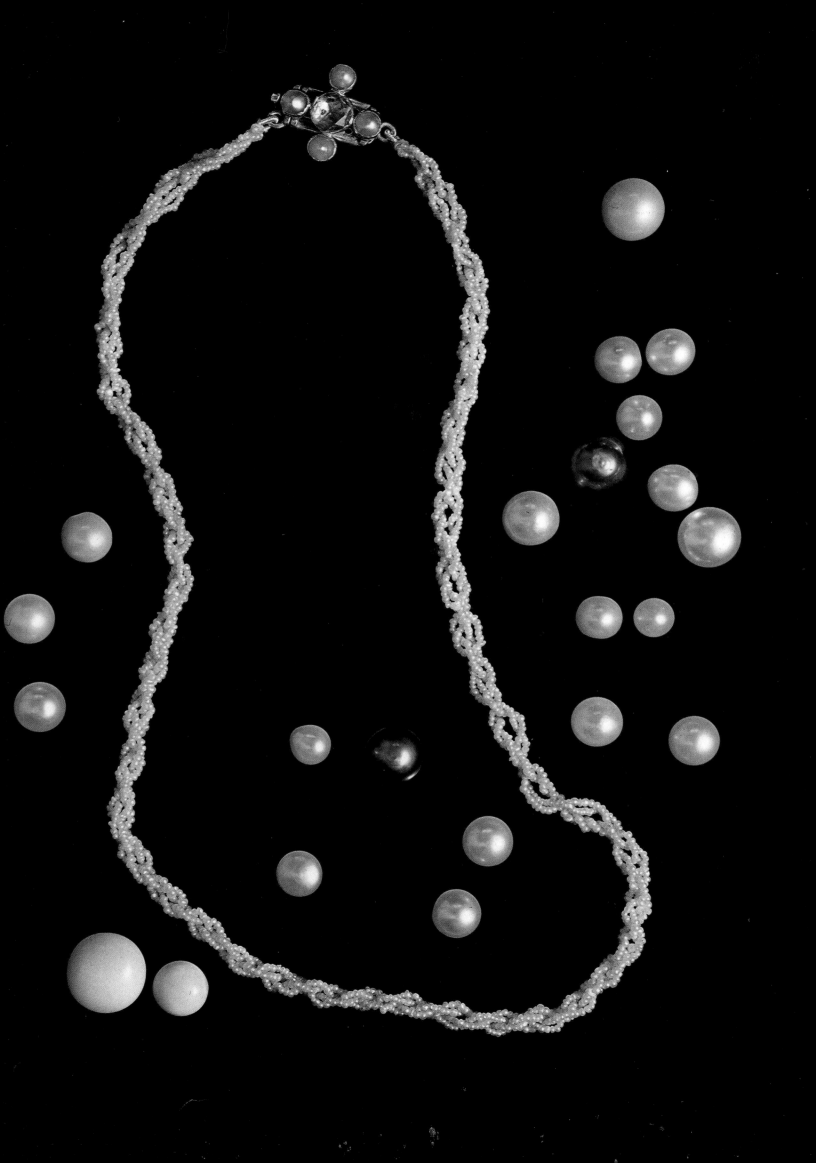

Below: *A Victorian tourmaline and split pearl cluster brooch c. 1850-60. A wide gold hinged bangle with split pearl and diamond cluster centre, circa 1870. (Bonhams Auctioneers)*

Above: *Brilliant cut diamond, and round and oval sapphire cluster bracelet and brilliant and baguette cut diamond, oval sapphire pendant on chain. (Garrard The Crown Jewellers)*

Below: *Pink topaz, pearl and gold cross with matching necklace. (Garrard The Crown Jewellers)*

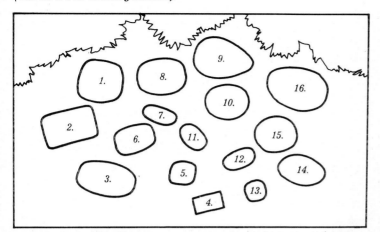

Below: *Selection of gems from E.A. Thompson (Gems) Ltd.*

1. *Tourmaline antique. 36.30 carat.*
2. *Green tourmaline. 28.30 carat.*
3. *Eilat oval.*
4. *Tourmaline bi-colour (pink & green). 3.45 carat.*
5. *Sapphire. 5.56 carat.*
6. *Precious topaz antique. 17.78 carat.*
7. *Fire opal. 3.15 carat.*
8. *Kunzite oval. 43.75 carat.*
9. *Citrine drop. 48.37 carat.*
10. *Blue topaz oval. 31.48 carat.*
11. *Sapphire ceylon. 9.03 carat.*
12. *Peridot oval. 6.72 carat.*
13. *Ruby. 3.44 carat.*
14. *Chrysoprase cabochon.*
15. *Garnet oval. 22.11 carat.*
16. *Amethyst oval. 54.87 carat.*

The unique lustre of pearls is mostly thought of in terms of creamy-white or faintly tinged with a pink glow. But these gems, too, can be fancy-coloured and come in definite shades of yellow, bronze, gunmetal, rose, green, blue and even black, the most romantic sounding of all, if a little melancholy.

Tourmaline is a jewel of many colours. It is probably best known when bottle-green or in varying shades of red, from pink to a deep, wine shade. As well as blue, brown and yellow, it is found in a lilac colour. Perhaps the most fascinating type of tourmaline is the 'watermelon'; this descriptive term calls it to mind immediately. The way the delicate pink and green colours are deposited conjures up this attractive fruit, as if by magic.

The blue of the sapphire is familiar largely because of

Below: *Diamond, blue enamel snake bangle with ruby eyes.*
(Philip Antrobus Ltd.)

Facing Page: *A Burma ruby, navette and brilliant diamond suite. (Asprey & Co. Ltd.)*

Above: *An embossed gold and chrysoprase set necklace. English mid-Victorian. (Cameo Corner Ltd.)*

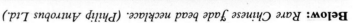

its popularity as an engagement ring, often framed in diamonds. The so-called 'star' sapphire is quite different, being an exquisite smoke-blue. The star-shape seen in its depths is caused by bunches of needle-like crystals, reflecting the light. The effect is emphasised by the smooth, dome-shape or cabochon cut, in which it usually appears.

Precious topaz, something of a rarity today, is recognizable when yellow-gold, honey-yellow or deep sherry. It also comes in other colours, all of them beautifully described by Oscar Wilde as "yellow as the eyes of a tiger, topazes as pink as the eyes of a wood pigeon, and green topazes that are as the eyes of a cat"; an excellent example of how colour can be caught and held by words.

As there is such a bewildering array of gemstone colours, it is difficult to recall them at will. Finding and remembering corresponding colours in living nature can ease this task and even heighten the enjoyment of unfamiliar stones.

For example, there is Labradorite, which belongs to the same group as Moonstone and is basically dark grey with flashes of green and blue, due to the play of light. A similarity can be drawn to the iridescence seen on the wings of some butterflies. In contrast there is the fresh apple green of Chrysoprase which looks its best in a necklace of beads. A number of these appetising

Facing Page, above: *A Burma ruby, navette and brilliant diamond brooch. (Asprey & Co. Ltd.)*

Facing Page, below: *Ruby, sapphire, and brilliant diamond bee on rhodochrosite dish. (Garrard The Crown Jewellers)*

Above: *Emerald and diamond suite set in 18 ct. gold. (Jewellery by Graff)*

Above: *A very fine emerald and diamond pendant on a diamond chain. Emerald 9.05 ct. (Asprey & Co. Ltd.)*

Left: *Round emerald centre, brilliant cut diamond border pendant with marquise and brilliant cut diamond and yellow gold chain. (Garrard The Crown Jewellers)*

Below: *Yellow gold emeralds and diamond necklace with two heart shaped emeralds and navette diamond clusters. (Cartier, London)*

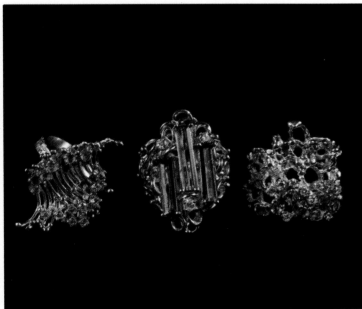

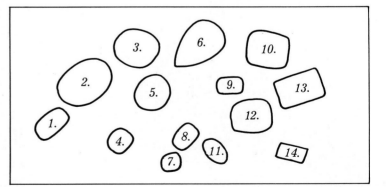

1. *Precious topaz antique. 17.78 carat.*
2. *Amethyst oval. 54.87 carat.*
3. *Kunzite oval. 43.75 carat.*
4. *Sapphire. 5.56 carat.*
5. *Blue Topaz oval. 31.48 carat.*
6. *Citrine drop. 48.37 carat.*
7. *Ruby. 3.44 carat.*
8. *Sapphire ceylon. 9.03 carat.*
9. *Peridot oval. 6.72 carat.*
10. *Tourmaline antique. 36.30 carat.*
11. *Fire opal. 3.15 carat.*
12. *Garnet oval. 22.11 carat.*
13. *Green tourmaline. 28.30 carat.*
14. *Tourmaline bi-colour (pink & green). 3.45 carat.*

gemstones need to be worn in order to show them off to their best advantage. Eilat stone captures two elements in its depths, giving the effect of a swirling, turquoise-coloured cloud, with moss green undertones. The frail pink of spring blossom is held forever in Rose quartz, while Citrine recalls autumn leaves, going from light golden-yellow to a reddish-yellow. Aquamarine, as the name suggests, mirrors sea shades, from pale blue to

With regard to the five principal gemstones, certain colours indicate those of finest quality. Blue-white is colour.

of good colour can cost more than a larger one of poor on the colour-quality. It is interesting to note that a gem colour and clarity. A great deal of importance is placed

The value of a gemstone depends on its carat-weight, together.

there is no disharmony when their colours are worn of jewellery. Gems seem to complement each other and that only gives delight to the eye. The same can be said happily. A herbaceous border shows an array of colours found in grass, leaves, shrubs and trees blend quite note in a garden where the various shades of green Natural colours do not clash. There is never a jarring assumes the red of a succulent raspberry.

quite definitely grass-green but under artificial light it colour within itself is the rare Alexandrite. By day it is clear green. A gem that shows a distinct change of

Left: *Pink sapphire and pearl pendant. (Philip Antrobus Ltd.)*

(Jewellery by Graff.)

Above: *Cabochon sapphire and diamond necklace.*

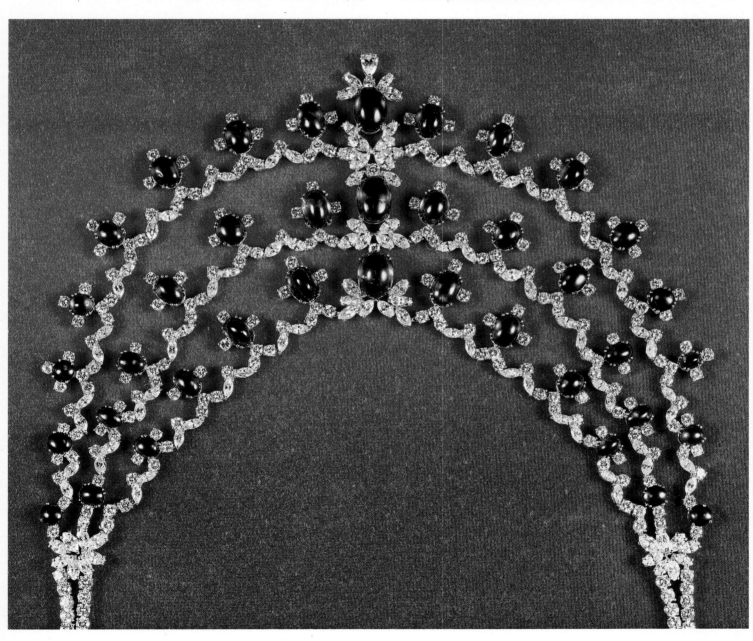

the top colour for a diamond. But it must be explained that this is really a contradiction in terms, for the blue-white should be completely colourless. It is, in fact, a trade description and accepted as such.

The most rare and valuable colour for a ruby is 'pigeon's blood' red. Where sapphires are concerned, the pale cornflower blue is considered to be the finest and not the dark-blue variety. A definite grass-green makes for a prize emerald and their scarcity adds to the worth of this variety. The choicest pearl is the rosé; it shows a pinky hue, which seems to emphasise the lustrous quality.

It is obvious that people who find a particular delight in the colours of nature should respond in equal measure to gemstones. However, unlike flowers, they never fade, but do have in common a depth and richness of colour.

There is a timeless quality about jewels that gives a feeling of mystery. Like trees they have taken centuries to evolve and have lain in the earth for so long, that when they are found, they appear to emerge like buried treasure.

Above: *Sapphire and diamond cluster ring mounted in 18 ct. white gold.*
Sapphire and diamond cluster ring mounted in 18 ct. yellow gold.
Sapphire and diamond cluster ring mounted in 18 ct. white gold.
(Garrard The Crown Jewellers)

Below: *Aquamarine, diamond and 18 ct. white gold necklace, aquamarine, and diamond cluster ring mounted in 18 ct. white gold. (Garrard The Crown Jewellers)*

2. Organic Gems

The lore of gemstones would not be complete without including a group of gems that owes its existence, not to minerals, but to something that was once alive: that is to say, an organism. These plant and animal products are further examples of the beauties of nature at another level.

It is well-known that pearls are found in oysters whose habitat is the sea and are the result of an irritant, for example a grain of sand. But there is another type called river or freshwater pearls, created by a certain pearl-bearing mussel, found in the rivers of the Northern Hemisphere, such as the Spey, the South Esk, the Forth, the Teith and Tay, in Scotland.

The pearl is probably the most important gem in this group. Among the earliest of known jewels it is the first to be mentioned in the translated writings of ancient Egypt and even then particular reference was made to its lustre.

The actual origin of the pearl has never been established and is lost in the dim ages past. Perhaps some primitive man who lived by the sea found one by accident when feeding from a particular shellfish.

Another unique aspect of the pearl is the fact that it is the only gem that does not need to be cut and polished,

Above: *Fine rosé pearl necklace with marquise diamond cluster clasp.* *(Edgar D. Truman)*

Left: *Section of a pearl tray used for assembling pearl necklaces.* *(Edgar D. Truman)*

but for certain items the pearl needs to be drilled or partly drilled. Indeed its natural lustre is so remarkable that it can often be taken straight from the shell for use in jewellery.

The pearl-producing oyster is a soft-bodied animal, more like a scallop than an edible oyster. It belongs to the Bivalve group of molluscs and the name means, simply, double-shell. Nature uses this shell to protect the soft mantle of the animal. Sometimes a sharp fragment penetrates the shell, like a grain of sand, a piece of broken shell or even a shell-boring animal. Consequently an irritation is set up and in an attempt to ease this annoyance, the oyster covers the irritant with a mother-of-pearl type substance, called nacre. The whole of the irritant within the tissue is completely enveloped. The oyster continues to add layers of this nacre, so that the more layers there are, the larger the pearl.

There is quite a variety of shapes in natural pearls. The perfectly spherical ones are ideal for necklets. The pear-shaped or so-called drop pearls make excellent earrings or pendants. The button shape, with one side somewhat flattened, seem to be designed specially for ear-studs. Mutated pearls, described as baroque, are beautiful oddities, as are tiny seed pearls which have never reached full maturity.

It is a sad fact that new supplies of natural pearls are so rare as to be practically non-existent. This is due to a number of reasons but the plain fact is a natural shortage brought about by pollution and the difficulty of finding divers. However, cultured pearls have now taken their place. Initially the irritant is introduced by hand, usually in the form of a shell bead. The process is something like planting a seed, for nature then takes over completely, determining the colour and size of the resultant pearl. In fact cultured pearls resemble an exotic hot-house plant, being cultivated on the same lines, in controlled circumstances.

Experiments in producing cultured pearls suitable for commercial use, were carried out in Japan from about 1899. But it was not until the 1920s that cultured pearls

Below: *A colour graduated coral bead and diamond suite. (Asprey & Co. Ltd.)*

Facing Page: *A coral, diamond and cultured black pearl necklace. (Asprey & Co. Ltd.)*

Below: *A mid-Victorian carved coral and gold ramshead brooch, Italian. (Cameo Corner Ltd.)*

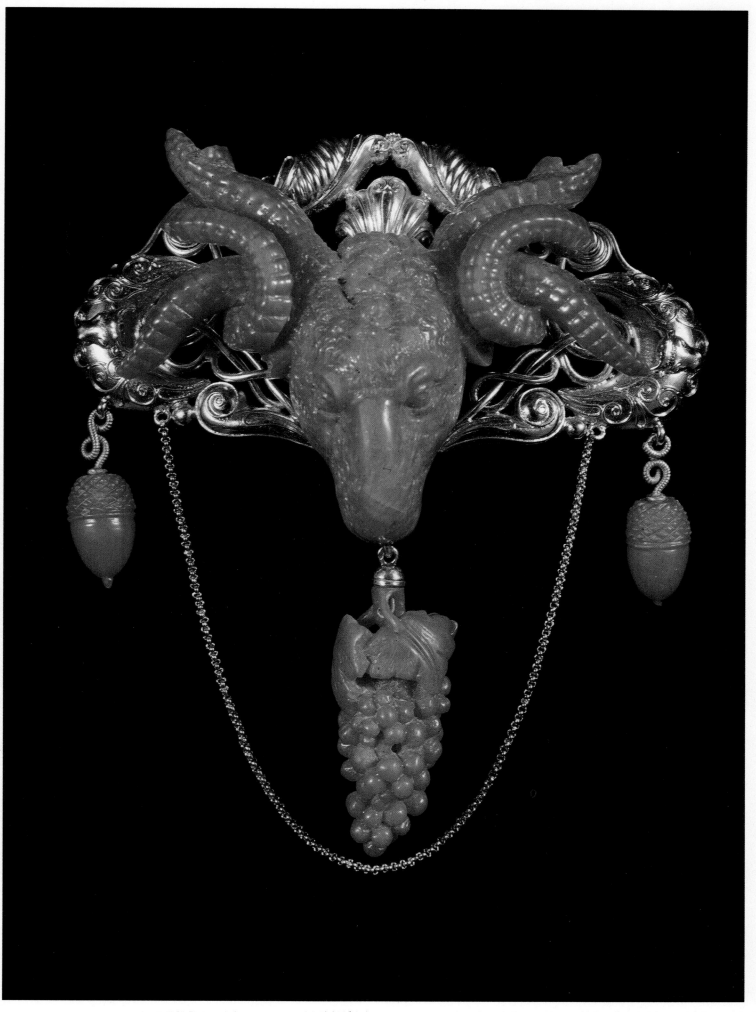

Left: *A coral and diamond pumpkin spray by Cartier of London. Circa 1930. (Hancocks & Co. Ltd.)*

came upon the general market to any extent. It must be noted that this way of artificiallly stimulating oysters was discovered by the Chinese as far back as the 13th century. They placed tiny carvings of Buddha inside the oyster, these were subsequently covered with nacre, and transformed into miniature mother-of-pearl ornaments.

Coral is basically the secretion from a tiny sea-creature called polyp. It uses this calcium carbonate substance to make a communal dwelling on the sea-bed, rather like scaffolding, thus providing an anchor for this boneless-type of animal whose primitive nature could be said to resemble a miniature form of sea-anemone.

Like the pearl, coral is a product of the sea. It has been dredged from the depths for centuries. It is thought that coral jewellery was first worn in Hellenistic Greece. The main source of this gem used to be the Mediterranean coast of Italy where Naples

Below: *A baguette and brilliant diamond necklace with an angel skin coral pendant. (Asprey & Co. Ltd.)*

Below Right: *Early 19th Century carved coral brooch (part of a set) of putti, mystical sea beasts and shells. Italian. (Cameo Corner Ltd.)*

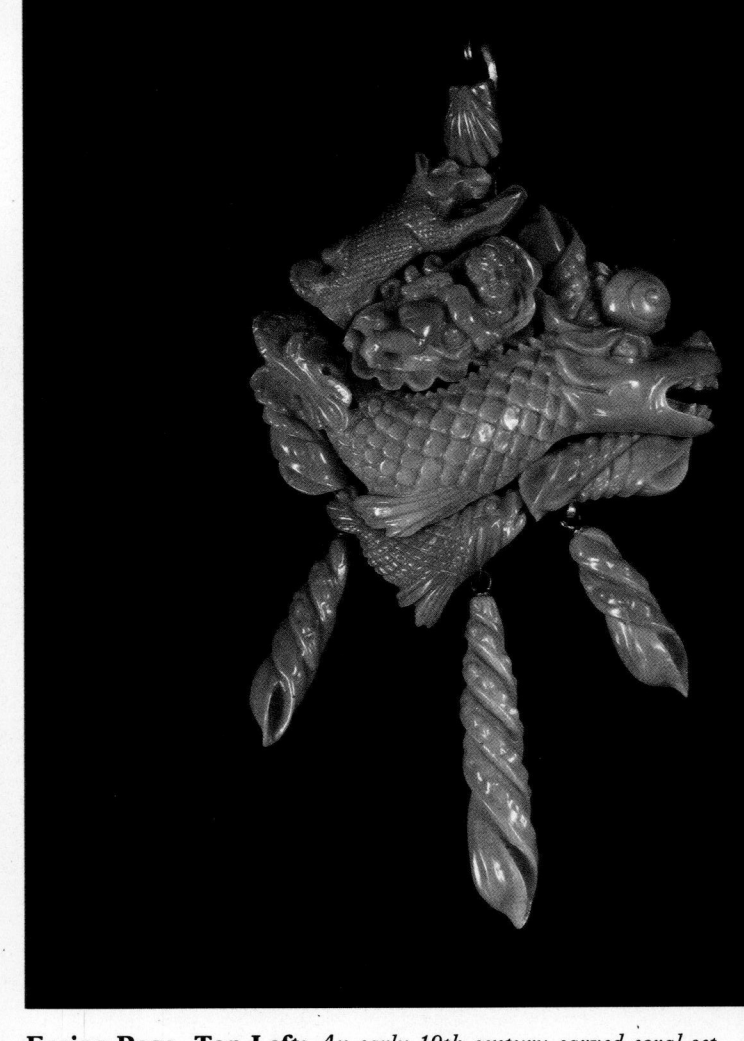

Facing Page, Top Left: *An early 19th century carved coral set of a necklace with matching brooch in the form of putti, shells and mystical sea beasts, Italian. (Cameo Corner Ltd.)*

Top Right: *Pendant necklet, carved rock crystal, coral and diamond mounted in 18 ct. yellow gold. (Mappin & Webb)*

Right: *Angel skin coral and sapphire necklace with matching earrings by Lacloche. (Collingwood of Conduit Street Ltd.)*

was the centre for the craft of coral carving. Today most of it comes from Japan and from the waters of the Mediterranean along the African and European coasts.

Coral comes in a diversity of colours: pure white, pale flesh pink known as angel's skin, pale and bright rose, salmon, red, dark red and ox-blood red. In ancient times soothsayers used coral beads as charms. They were said to be a protection against shipwrecks, fire, lightning and whirlwinds. The Romans hung beads of red coral around the necks of babies or decorated their cradles with them. They believed that coral would preserve their teeth and ensure that they never worked loose. They also thought that the babies would be protected from falling sickness and fits and that evil spirits would never come near because the jangling of the coral beads would frighten them away.

There was a great demand for coral in the Victorian period. Sometimes it was left in its branch-like state. The pale-pink variety was usually carved into delicate flowers. For added detail each leaf and petal was separately worked.

A very acceptable gift for a baby girl in Victorian times was a coral necklace. The colour was thought to attract a child and the beads could not be easily broken as this natural substance resembles the composition of teeth. Perhaps that is why coral beads were also used as baby teethers.

Amber is the fossilised resin exuded from a certain type of prehistoric pine tree which flourished before the

Above: *An early 19th century Italian filigree gold necklet in the Etruscan manner with a central cameo of a negro's head, with rose cut diamond set collar. Made by Pallotti. (Cameo Corner Ltd.)*

Below: *Angel skin coral, diamond and sapphire necklace by Lacloche. (Collingwood of Conduit Street Ltd.)*

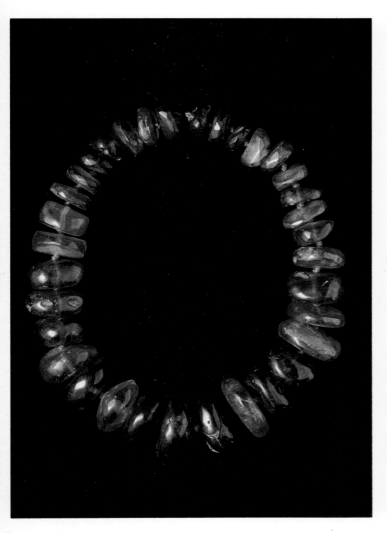

Above: *Ancient tomb necklace of Burmese amber circa 16th century. (Sac Freres)*

Below: *Chinese carvings of Baltic, Persian, and Burmese amber, early 19th century. (Sac Freres)*

Above: *Mandarin necklace of Persian amber, carved in China. Period Chien Lunj, 18th century. (Sac Freres)*

great Ice Age, more than thirty million years ago. A variety of insects, pieces of moss, tufts of lichens, pine needles and even lizards were caught and held in the amber as it oozed down the pine tree, in a soft and sticky state, to preserve them forever. The allusion to 'a fly in amber' can therefore be considered a fact and not merely a saying.

Amber has been known and valued since the beginning of recorded time. Early civilizations made rings from it before the introduction of the more sophisticated precious metals. The tree from which precious amber comes, the pinus succinfera, is now extinct. But the name *succinum* is Latin for amber, so the word association persists even after an incredible passage of time. The Baltic coast is its most important source. At Kalingrad, in the U.S.S.R., there is a museum which houses a remarkable collection of 50,000 specimens of amber, some containing centuries old flora and fauna.

Amber colours have a remarkable fascination. There is a warm tone of pale yellow, a deeply glowing orange and a rich, dark reddish-brown. In the 1880s, when the Aesthetic reaction against the ornate and over-decorative set in, a plain string of beautifully coloured amber beads was the only acceptable adornment.

Jet also comes from trees, dating back to the primeval age. One school of thought suggests that the trees involved were of the Monkey Puzzle variety. Jet is another fossil, in this case a fossilised wood, closely related to coal. Obtained from driftwood, it is a form of

Above: *Large rare hand cut faceted necklace of Baltic amber, 18th century, worn by a member of the late Russian imperial court. (Sac Freres)*

Below: *Baltic amber fish carved in China early 19th century. (Sac Freres)*

Below: *Late 19th century jet cameo and vulcanite bracelet. English. (Cameo Corner Ltd.)*

brown coal which has been subjected to long periods of exposure to chemical action in stagnant water. Finally, great pressures were brought to bear which caused it to flatten into the familiar substance known as jet.

There is a possibility that the name, jet, is derived from its place of origin, Gagee or Gagas, along the Mediterranean coast of Asia Minor. The Romans had a great love of jet so that, subsequently, this became their main source of supply.

Jet has been found in early burial mounds throughout

Above: *A group of carved Whitby jet jewellery including a foliated bracelet, a cameo bangle, and an important pair of earrings. English, late 19th century. (Cameo Corner Ltd.)*

Great Britain. These discoveries, in the form of beads, pendants and charms, indicate the existence of jet even before recorded history.

The ancient seaport of Whitby, in Yorkshire, was famous for the high quality of jet found there and for the industry that flourished as far back as Roman times, reaching its peak of popularity during the Mid-Victorian period. By the beginning of the 20th century the industry declined and now there is only a museum at Whitby where examples of the craftsman's art may be seen. Delicately carved birds, butterflies and insects decorate such items as brooches, bracelets, earrings and half ornaments.

Jet was particularly useful as mourning jewellery. On the death of Prince Albert, Queen Victoria plunged the Court into deepest mourning. For a year only black was allowed to be worn and even coloured gemstones were banned. Consequently jet assumed an important role in the fashion of the day. This vogue was emphasised by the Queen's subjects who slavishly followed her example in most things. Of course their somewhat macabre interest in death found appropriate expression in this sombre gem.

Jet is still found in Spain and France. No longer worked on a regular basis, it has assumed a certain rarity as a gem material.

3. A Golden Compliment to Gemstones

The essential beauty and colour of gemstones seem to be intensified when set in the sun-glow of gold. This precious metal has had an almost hypnotic quality through the ages. For over 6,000 years it has inspired men to wage war, amass wealth and to demonstrate their love of women. This last has found expression in jewellery, where it pays a particular compliment to gemstones.

Apparently there is no common derivation for the word gold. The Greek term came from the Hebrew, to shine, and this definition applies to Sanskrit and the Teutonic languages, where it also means a shining or a glowing metal. Perhaps the most charming allusion to its origin lies in the Latin word for gold, which is aurum; related to the Italian, aurora, meaning morning glow or shining dawn, it conjures up a romantic image of gold.

Gold was probably the first metal to be worked by primitive man and certain evidence indicates that it was known to the early Egyptians and Babylonians, right back to the beginning of recorded history. The warm glow of gold must have attracted early man as it lay in glittering particles in the sandy bed of many rivers. As gold is heavier than most other metals, the sand could be washed away, leaving grains and chips of gold behind. Its scarcity and mystical appeal, as a symbol of power, gave it divine attributes. According to legend gold was said to be the child of Zeus, father of the gods, and as such could adorn the walls of the temples and be

Above: *18 ct. yellow gold, ruby, diamond and pearl set mask pendant on 18 ct. yellow gold chain. (Carrington)*

Left: *A filigree mounted enamelled pendant of a peasant scene. Dutch 17th century. (Cameo Corner Ltd.)*

offered as a sacrifice to the gods.

The legend of the Golden Fleece concerns Jason and his band of heroes, the Argonauts. After many perilous adventures, Jason finally secured the Golden Fleece, helped by Medea, with whom he subsequently spent ten stormy years. Jason then married the daughter of King Creon and his untimely end is said to have come about while resting in the shade of his ship, the Argo. The poop fell upon him and accidently crushed him to death.

There is possibly a practical explanation to part of this legend. The Golden Fleece could, indeed, have been nothing more than a sheepskin, commonly used in ancient times to trap the fine specks of alluvial gold found in the fast flowing waters of certain streams.

Known as the noblest precious metal, gold is

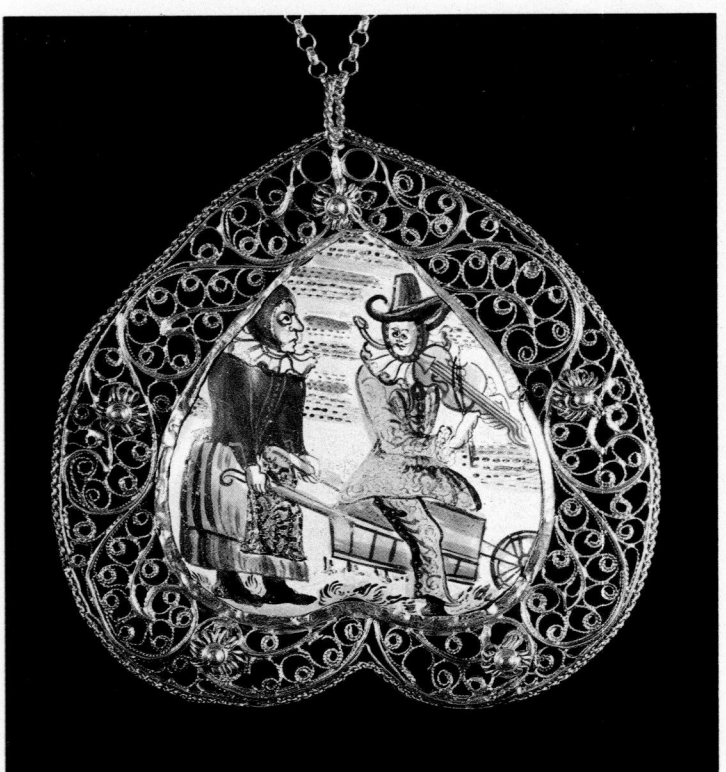

Above: *Emerald and diamond gold brooch pendant with gold chain. (Philip Antrobus Ltd.)*

Below: *Two 18 ct. yellow gold, diamond set birds with drop ruby foliage. (Carrington)*

Left: *18 ct. yellow gold owl pendant on chain with diamond head and onyx eyes. (Carrington)*

Overleaf: *Diamond crystals, brilliant cut diamond, and yellow gold suite consisting of earrings, ring, necklace. (Garrard The Crown Jewellers)*

indestructible, neither tarnishing nor corroding. Gold coins have been recovered from treasure ships lost beneath the sea for two centuries, still looking as bright as new.

The early Egyptians used the circle to symbolise divinity, perfection and the sun. As they considered gold to be the most perfect of metals, it was also represented by the circle. Alchemists called gold, sol, the sun or Apollo and designated it as such by means of a crown of rays, referring to it as the very King, or Apollo of metals.

The art of goldsmithing had reached a height of excellence by about 3,000 B.C., not only in Egypt, where gold was found quite extensively, but also in Mesopotamia where it was traded. A remarkable example of the goldsmith's art can be seen in a beautifully tooled helmet found at Ur and dating from about 2700 B.C. Another treasure is the lid of Tutankhamun's coffin, made in his image with incredible artistry, about 1350 B.C.

In these early days only Kings and the very rich were able to use gold but it became more plentiful so its use

Above: *Cat pendant with marquise cut diamond eyes. 18 ct. oxydised white gold mask. (Garrard The Crown Jewellers)*

Below: *9 ct. gold fairy pendant and butterfly earrings. (Booty Jewellery)*

Below: *18 ct. gold and diamond necklace. (Kutchinsky)*

increased. In general terms smaller articles of jewellery appeared and it was possible for more people to become the owners of such treasured possessions.

Gold has been found in Britain; in fact there is a goldmine in North Wales which is unfortunately no longer commercially worthwhile. It is interesting to note that every royal bride of this century has been married with a wedding ring made from the gold of this Welsh mine.

It has a characteristic colour, being reddish-yellow with a green tinge.

Gold in its pure state is unsuitable for making into jewellery and has to be alloyed, that is mixed with other metals, to give the required hardness and desired colour, ranging from yellow to purple. Indeed the demand from various markets throughout the world and prevailing fashions have a marked influence on the

Above: *Sculptured 18ct gold rings, pendants and bracelets by Björn Weckström. (Booty Jewellery)*

Left: *18 ct. yellow gold robin pendant on chain, set with rubies. (Carrington)*

production of the various gold colours. At one time Europeans preferred a redder gold than the British. Of late there is a noticeable swing towards white gold, both in Britain and abroad. Multi-coloured gold has become popular, and this entails a mixture of red, yellow and white, but more extravagant shades have been produced to include green, lilac, blue and purple.

Of course the quality of gold is of the utmost importance. In Britain there are four legal standards: 22-carat, 18-carat, 14-carat and 9-carat. In other countries 8-carat and 15-carat are legal. This carat system is a way of indicating the proportion of gold there is to the other metals in a particular alloy. Pure gold is reckoned as 24 carat, therefore 22-carat will contain 22 parts of gold to two parts of other metal. 18-carat has 18 parts of gold to 6 parts of other metal. 14-carat gold is not often used in this country but to

Above: *Yellow gold, diamond set in navette shape motives.*
(Cartier, Paris)

estimate it, the count is 14 parts of gold to 10 parts of other metal. Where 9-carat gold is concerned, there are 9 parts of gold and 15 parts of other metal.

British hallmarks have acted as safeguard to purchasers of gold, and of course silver, for over six centuries. In 1300 King Edward I gave the responsibility for testing and certifying the quality of precious metals to the Worshipful Company of Goldsmiths.

The Goldsmith's Company came into existence in London during the 12th century. It was originally a 'getting together' of the goldsmiths, silversmiths and jewellers so that they could protect themselves and provide financial aid for their families. A central fund was formed to which subscriptions were allocated. Their first building was erected in 1340, near St. Paul's Cathedral and they have been on the same site ever since.

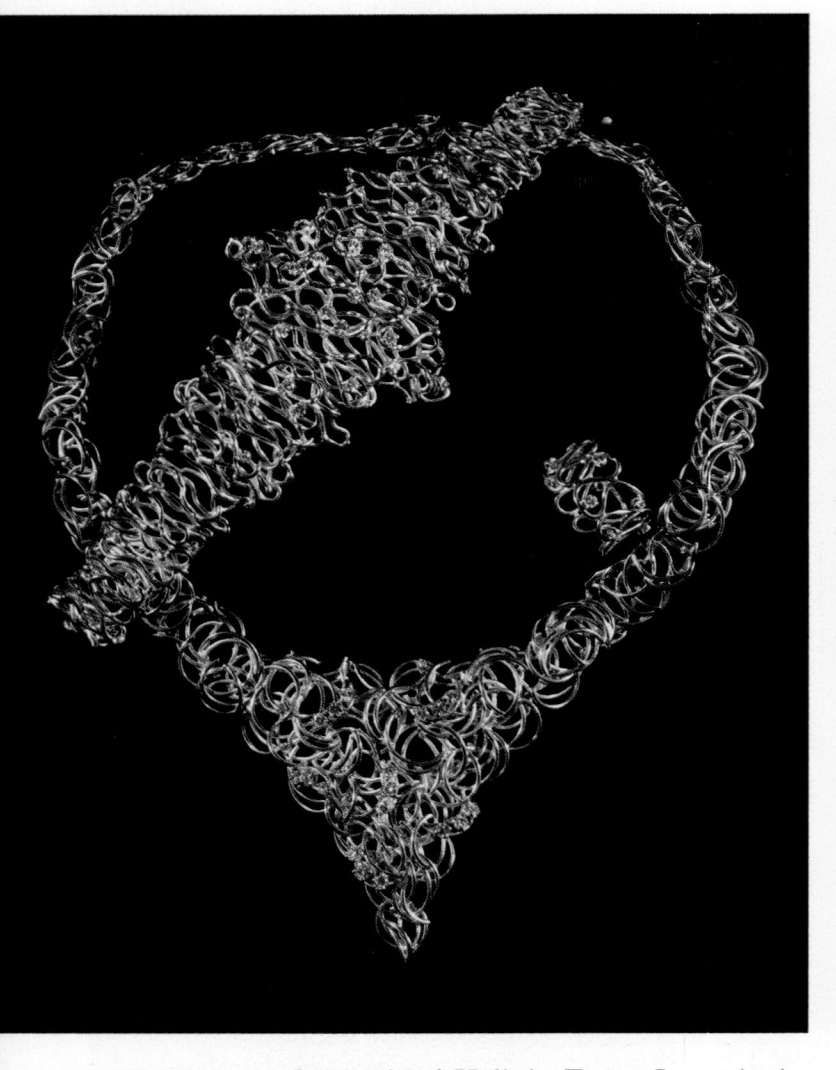

Left: *Necklace, bracelet and ring, 18 ct. gold wire sculpture set with brilliant cut diamonds. (Mappin & Webb)*

Above: *9 ct. multi-coloured gold bracelet, 18 ct. gold woven mesh bracelet, 18 ct. gold and quartz necklace, 18 ct. yellow and white gold bracelet. (Garrard The Crown Jewellers)*

The present Goldsmiths' Hall, in Foster Lane, is the fourth and was completed in 1835. Since they were appointed 'Guardians of the Craft' in 1300, the Goldsmiths' Company have controlled the testing and marking of gold and silver objects. Hallmarking, the world's oldest form of consumer protection, takes its name from their hall, which still houses the London Assay Office. There are now three more British Assay Offices, in Birmingham, Sheffield and Edinburgh, although there were other Assay Offices in former times.

Hallmarks are a definite form of protection for they show that an article has been tested at an Assay Office and certify that the metal used conforms to one of the legal standards of fineness and purity. British Assay Offices are incorporated by Royal Charter or by statute and all are independent of any trade organisation. This guarantee of quality ensures the highest standards of gold as used in jewellery.

Gold plays an essential part in the design concept of jewellery. It is not the amount that matters: it is the way it is used. The response of gold is quite remarkable. Easy to handle, it lends itself to carving, chiselling and melting. It can also be wrought into delicate tendrils and twigs or further enriched with golden granules. Tiny squares can be applied in such a way as to produce different levels.

Gold wire used in contemporary designs has its origins in the early Italian or Etruscan period. Another way with gold is to have slender twisted ropes made into rings, bracelets and brooches. In the time of Tutankhamun, Egyptian goldsmiths created their gold jewellery in similar fashion.

Textured gold, with a bark or frosted finish, has added interest and is probably more practical to wear because it eliminates fingermarks and conceals scratches. Combined with high polished gold a mixture of the two makes for a greater play of light and shade. Many of the larger and more imposing pieces of gold jewellery revert to the polished surface and this seems to intensify the depth of this fascinating precious metal.

Much of the variation in jewellery design relies on the versatility of gold and its apparent ease of manipulation. Spanning the centuries it has been an adornment almost since the dawn of history, thus preserving the traditional as well as the romantic aspects. Its inherent characteristic is a golden glow that gives a feeling of warmth at all times.

Right: *18 ct. gold bracelet, 18 ct. gold and quartz necklace, 18 ct. yellow and white gold bracelet, 18 ct. gold bangle, 9 ct. multi-coloured gold necklace, 9 ct. multi-coloured gold bracelet, 18 ct. gold and pearl ring, 18 ct. gold woven mesh bracelet, 18 ct. gold neckchain. (Garrard The Crown Jewellers)*

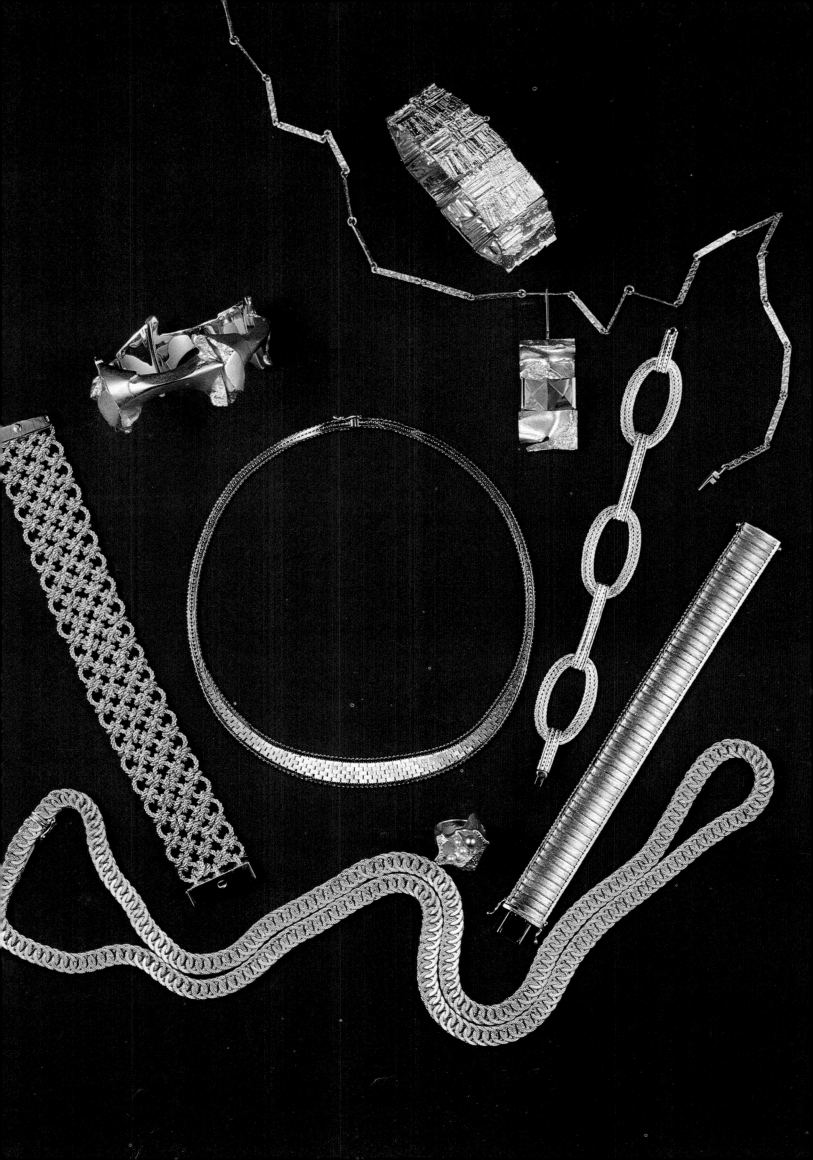

4. Birthstones of the Month

Ever since the beginning of recorded history, there is evidence that people have needed something to strengthen their confidence in the future and in themselves. For centuries Birthstones have been thought of as a personal talisman of particular beauty and interest. Indeed these gems were said to emphasise certain qualities within a person, so that they could live a more serene life, secure in the knowledge that the Birthstone would protect them from evil.

Exodus. The twelve gems were arranged in four rows of three stones each and were subsequently linked with the twelve signs of the Zodiac. It is interesting to note that almost the same twelve stones are recorded in Revelations, the final book of the New Testament, as the stones in the foundation of the wall of the Heavenly Jerusalem.

Below: *An early Victorian frosted gold carbuncle and seed pearl fob brooch, English. (Cameo Corner Ltd.)*

Above: *Birthstones of the Month —
E.A. Thomson (Gems) Limited*

January	—	Garnet	July	—	Ruby
February	—	Amethyst	August	—	Peridot
March	—	Aquamarine	September	—	Sapphire
April	—	Diamond	October	—	Opal
May	—	Emerald	November	—	Topaz
June	—	Pearl	December	—	Turquoise

(Diamond supplied by D. & P. Clark (diamonds) Limited)

The idea of associating a special gem with each month was possibly suggested by the original breastplate worn by Aaron, High Priest of the Hebrews. It was made by Aaron's brother, Moses, about 1250 B.C., according to instructions he received during his forty days on the mountains, as recorded in

Of course, the original list of Birthstones has altered down the ages, due to difficulties in translation, changing values, scarcity and even the discovery of new gems. But there is a link with history among the Birthstones held today and they are the turquoise, the garnet and the amethyst, all dating back thousands of years B.C.

The current list of Birthstones was drawn up in 1912 by the National Association of Goldsmiths, in conjunction with their American counterpart. Each calendar month is covered by one particular Birthstone, unlike the Zodiacal version which affects only certain periods of the month and of the one following.

The gems chosen to represent the Birthstones of the Month in use today, have the greatest influence in Zodiacal terms, so that historic beliefs and legends can be applied without amendment.

Above: *Necklace and ring, carved rock crystal, set with amethysts, and diamonds mounted in 18 ct. yellow gold. (Mappin & Webb)*

Right: *Marquise diamond 26.73 ct. on diamond chain. (Jewellery by Graff)*

Below: *18 ct. gold, diamond and amethyst necklace. (Kutchinsky)*

The JANUARY Birthstone is the GARNET. The qualities it enhances are loyalty and a light heart. It is found in South Africa, Australia, Brazil, Sri Lanka and North America. In Medieval times the garnet was said to protect the wearer from all manner of poisons, cure depression and prevent nightmares.

The FEBRUARY Birthstone is the AMETHYST. The qualities it enhances are authority and peace of mind. Found in Sri Lanka, Madagascar, South America and the United States of America it is alleged to have been St. Valentine's favourite stone, who's amethyst ring was engraved with a cupid.

The MARCH Birthstone is the AQUAMARINE. The qualities it enhances are bravery and unchanging love. It is found in Madagascar, the U.S.S.R, Brazil, the United States of America and Burma. As its name suggests, the aquamarine has long been considered the sailor's gem. It ensured safe and prosperous voyages and was an added safeguard against the perils of the sea and the monsters of the deep.

The APRIL Birthstone is the DIAMOND. The qualities it enhances are caution and harmony in marriage. It is found in Southern Africa, West Africa, Central Africa, South America and the U.S.S.R. The ancient Greeks had a tremendous regard for diamonds. They maintained that wearing a diamond would end delirium, banish worries, curb violent feeling and strengthen love.

Overleaf: *Three tier diamond necklace set in 18 ct. white gold containing three major heart-shaped diamonds. (Jewellery by Graff)*

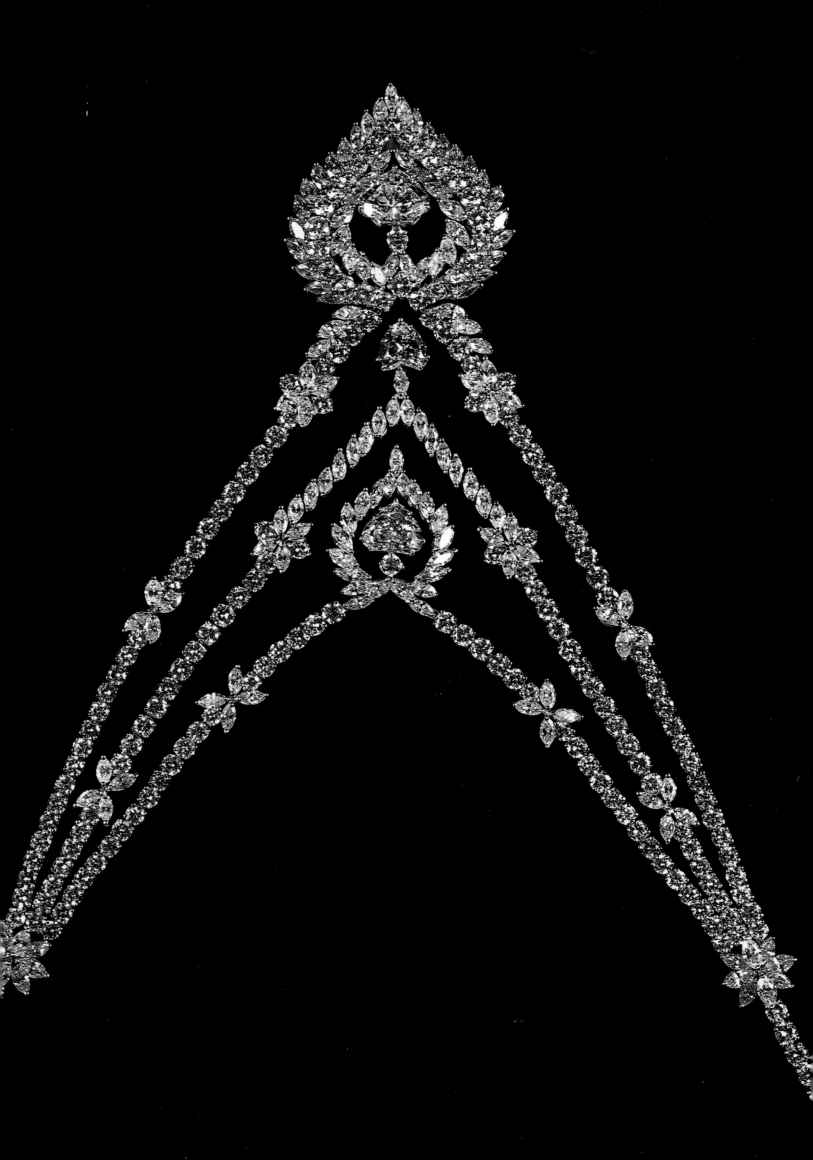

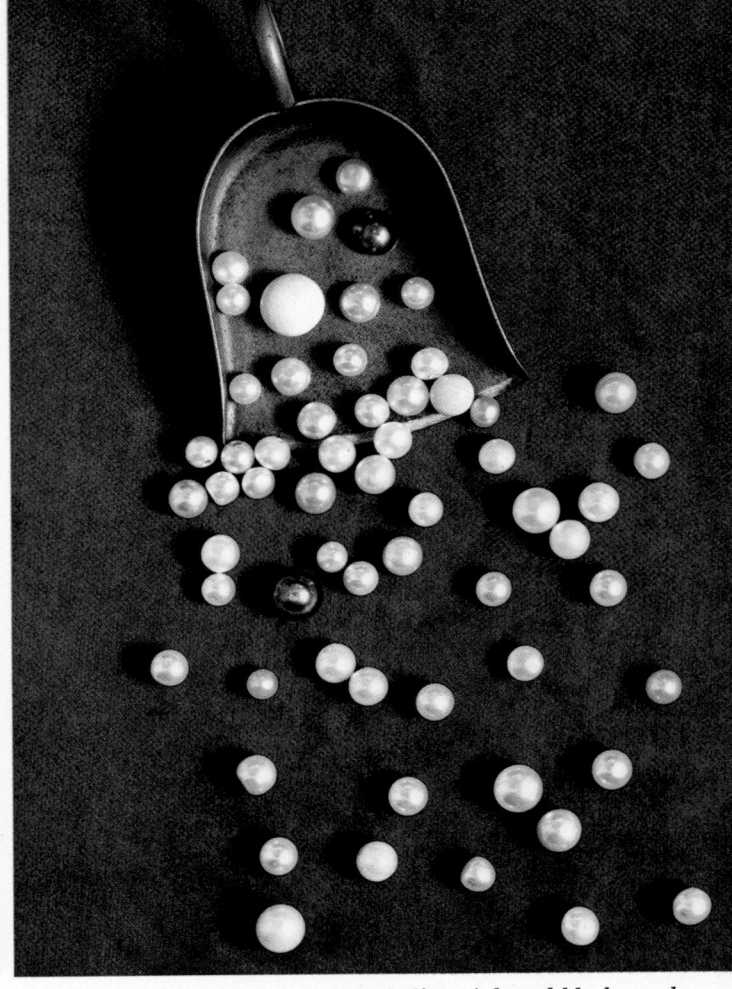

The MAY Birthstone is the EMERALD. The qualities it enhances are warm affection and the ability to succeed. It is found in Brazil, Colombia, India, South Africa and the U.S.S.R. During the Middle Ages the gem craftsmen of those days were said to find rest for their eyes if they looked at an emerald from time to time.

The JUNE Birthstone is the PEARL. The qualities it enhances are health and a charm of manner. It is found in the Persian Gulf, Sri Lanka and the North-West coast of Australia. As natural pearls are now almost unobtainable, cultured pearls are found mainly in Japan. A somewhat bizarre and extravagent toast was drunk to Queen Elizabeth I by her financial advisor, Sir Thomas Gresham. This was on the occasion of her visit to the Foreign Exchange when Sir Thomas had a pearl, of immense value in those days, crushed into a goblet of wine so that he could pledge his sovereign's health.

The JULY Birthstone is the RUBY. The qualities it enhances are devotion and true contentment. Found in Burma, Thailand and Sri Lanka, the ancient Orientals considered the ruby to be particularly luminous and referred to it as the 'glowing stone' or 'lamp stone'. Much later a Greek legend told of Hera, the Greek goddess of marriage and how she befriended a lame female stork. The stork showed her appreciation by bringing a ruby in her beak and putting it in the lap of her mistress; it was of such intense brilliance that Hera used it as a lamp at night while she walked on Mount Olympus.

Previous page: *Brilliant cut diamond and drop diamond cluster necklace. (Garrard The Crown Jewellers)*

Top Left: *Bangle with pavé-set diamond, set in 18 ct. gold. (Jewellery by Graff)*

Above: *Emerald and diamond suite set in 18 ct. yellow gold. (Jewellery by Graff)*

Above: *Oval and round peridot and brilliant cut diamond suite mounted in yellow gold consisting of necklace, earrings and ring. (Garrard The Crown Jewellers)*

Below: *Ruby, brilliant and navette diamond necklace, bracelet and ring. (Collingwood of Conduit Street Ltd.)*

The AUGUST Birthstone is the PERIDOT. The qualities it enhances are fidelity and amiability. Found in Burma, Sri Lanka, the Red Sea, Norway and the United States of America, the Romans wore it to ward of stark terror, spells and melancholy. In the Middle Ages the greatest fears were of the evil eye and of darkness.

The SEPTEMBER Birthstone is the SAPPHIRE. The qualities it enhances are sincerity and a sunny nature. It is found in Australia, Kalimantan, Burma, Sri Lanka, Kashmir, Thailand and the United States of America. During the Middle Ages the sapphire was the symbol of purity. It would therefore prevent impure thoughts and protect the priests from temptations of the flesh. In the thirteenth and fourteenth centuries popes, cardinals and bishops wore rings set with sapphires. This was most appropriate because the pure blue colour symbolised the heavens.

The OCTOBER Birthstone is the OPAL. The qualities it enhances are hope and good fortune. Found in Australia, Czechoslovakia and Mexico, the opal has been prized since ancient times. An Indian legend tells of the gods Brahma, Vishnu and Shiva and how they vied with each other for the love of a beautiful woman. Driven by jealous anger, unknown to each other, they changed her into a creature of the mist. In order to recognise her, each god gave the woman his own colour.

Below: Ring, ballerina cluster of one oval sapphire and baguette and brilliant cut diamonds mounted in 18 ct. white gold. (Mappin & Webb)

Above: Oval peridot and diamond leaf necklace on 18 ct. yellow gold chain. (Garrard The Crown Jewellers)

Above: *Opal in a delicate diamond and platinum millegrain setting. English: Circa 1920. (Hancocks & Co. Ltd.)*

Below: *Persian turquoise and diamond set in 18 ct. gold. (Jewellery by Graff)*

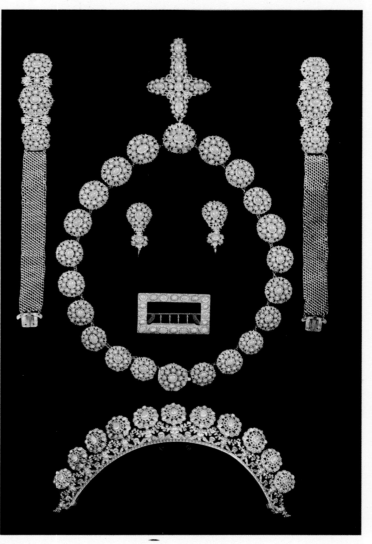

Right: Pink topaz, pearl and gold cross with matching necklace. (Garrard The Crown Jewellers)

Above: An important early 19th century suite of gold cannetille work set with turquoise comprising: a tiara, necklet with cruciform pendant, pair of earrings, pair of bracelets, and belt buckle. French or English. (Cameo Corner Ltd.)

Brahma gave her a heavenly blue, Vishnu enriched her with gold and Shiva added flaming red. But all this was in vain because the lovely wraith was whisked away by the winds. However, the gods did not want to lose her forever, so with their combined force they transformed her into the opal which reflects the colours of the rainbow.

The NOVEMBER Birthstone is the TOPAZ. The qualities it enhances are long life and intelligence. It is found in Australia, Brazil, Mexico, the U.S.S.R. and the United States of America. In ancient times the topaz was known as the 'stone of strength' because it was thought to derive certain powers from the sun. Kings and princes wore it in the belief that it endowed them with authority and wealth.

In the case of this particular Birthstone the CITRINE can be worn as an alternative. Precious topaz is seldom used in modern jewellery because of its increasing rarity.

The DECEMBER Birthstone is the TURQUOISE. The qualities it enhances are prosperity and an optimistic outlook. Found in Iran, Egypt, South America, the United States of America and the U.S.S.R., this is one of the earliest known gemstones and was found in the Sinai mines of Egypt, which are the oldest mines in the world, although inactive for the last three thousand years. The oldest recorded pieces of jewellery were found in 1900 at the tomb of Queen Zer who ruled about 5500 B.C. They are in the form of four magnificent bracelets.

5. Legends and Superstitions

The magic and mystery of gemstones are caught and held in the age-old legends and superstitions that still exist today. For every unattractive superstition there is a pleasant one to counteract it and that is how it should be, for jewellery is surely an expression of love, whether given as a present or bequeathed as a memento.

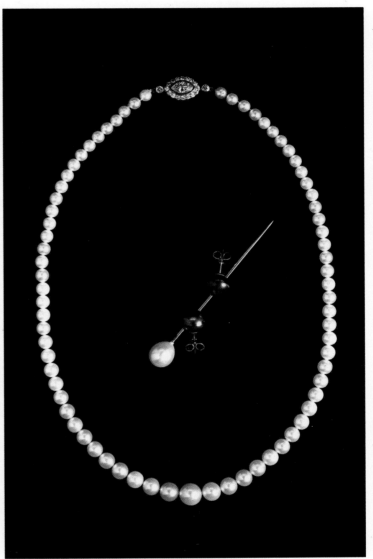

Below Left: *Brilliant cut diamond, opal centre cluster brooch mounted in yellow gold. (Garrard The Crown Jewellers)*

Below: *Fine rosé pearl necklace, drop pearl pin and a pair of black earstuds. (Edgar D. Truman)*

The folklore of gemstones would make an enormous tapestry, unfortunately too vast to recreate, but certain legends merit being picked out because of their universal interest.

The opal is probably the gem that is most talked of in the context of ill-luck and there is a simple explanation as to how this may have come about. In 1829 Sir Walter Scott wrote a novel called ANNE OF GEIERSTEIN, much of it concerning the Lady Hermione. She always wore a certain gem in her hair when she appeared on the social scene, because it seemed to have the magic power of emphasising her grace and vitality and when she removed it, these qualities faded. This gem was also influenced by her moods and shone more brightly when she was happy or blazed with colour when she was angry. Her great fear was that liquid might ruin the jewel and this caused a rival to accuse her of witchcraft. In order to quash the rumour, Lady Hermione's husband took her to a service in the family chapel and insisted on sprinkling her forehead with holy water. The worst happened. A drop fell on the gemstone, it shot forth a brilliant flash like a falling star, then instantly changed into a common pebble. Hermione fell dead on the chapel floor and both she and the gem became a heap of ashes.

Although Sir Walter Scott never mentioned the actual name of the gem, certain characteristics were described to make readers think in terms of the opal. Because Sir Walter Scott was as influential in his day as

Overleaf: *A 20th century cast silver gilt turquoise, garnet and pearl necklet with pendant depicting St George and the dragon in the Renaissance style. Mid-European. (Cameo Corner Ltd.)*

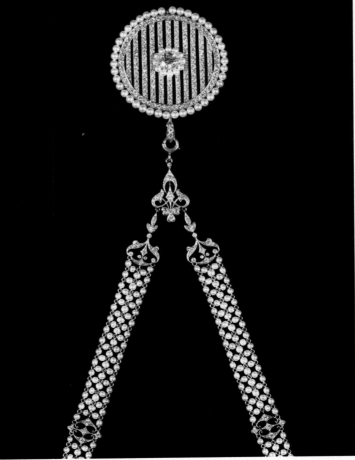

Above: *Marquise and brilliant cut diamond cluster necklace.*
(Garrard The Crown Jewellers)

Below: *Diamond choker set in yellow gold.* (Jewellery by Graff)

Facing Page: *Antique diamond necklace comprising clusters, drops and swags with matching brooch.*
(Collingwood of Conduit Street Ltd.)

Below: *A pearl and diamond "sautoire". Circa 1920.*
(Asprey & Co. Ltd.)

Previous page: *A contemporary collar by Gillian Tait, consisting of gold mounted mother-of-pearl discs, inset with various cabochon cut stones, including tourmalines, moonstones, opals, garnets and pearls.*
(Cameo Corner Ltd.)

are the press and television today, the story was so widely spread that the sale of opals declined for many years after its publication. However, a superstition going back to Roman Times maintains that the opal was probably one of the luckiest of gems. Its colours are the same as those seen in the rainbow, recognised by the Romans to be the symbol of hope, as it is today. This ancient belief is surely most appropriate for the modern world.

A legend that may explain why pearls are associated with tears dates back to the days of early Christianity. The simple people of those times had no knowledge as to the origin of pearls and thought they were the tears of angels shed for the sins of mankind and lodged in the depths of the sea. Moslems believe that the trees of paradise are hung with pearls, as told in the Koran. Long ago Arabs and Persians thought that pearls would help cure insanity.

Left: Demantoid garnet, ruby and brilliant diamond lizard brooch, emerald, ruby and brilliant diamond dragonfly brooch, sapphire, ruby and brilliant diamond bee brooch.
(Garrard The Crown Jewellers)

The first use of diamonds is presumed to be India where tiny diamonds were sprinkled over a baby's head at its naming ceremony. By so doing, the child assumed the qualities of virtue and purity. This gemstone has the legendary power of protecting the wearer from evil, especially when worn on the left side. This belief could have added to its popularity as an engagement ring. Diamonds are bound up with love and marriage and it is said that the gift of a diamond will 'quicken the

Above: Marquise and brilliant cut diamond cluster bracelet.
(Garrard The Crown Jewellers)

affection and restore love between husband and wife'.

There is a delightful and encouraging legend connected with the ruby. In the 13th century the then King of Siam was said to own a fabulous ruby, the size of a man's hand, and it was thought to have the power of prolonging youth. Each night and morning the King rubbed the priceless ruby over his face and neck. He died at the age of ninety and still had the complexion of a young man, without a blemish or wrinkle.

The Middle Ages abounded with superstitions about gemstones. It was thought that the power of a ruby was so great that, if placed in a bowl of cold water, its inner heat would make the water boil. Conversely, the topaz was said to chill boiling water in an instant.

During the Renaissance the topaz was held to have the unusual power of giving light in the dark, so much so, that a topaz owned by a Dutch count was known to light up the chapel where it was kept with such brilliance that prayers could be read without the aid of a lamp. Pursuing the idea that gemstones could provide light, there is a legend that Noah lit the Ark by means

Above: Cabouchon rubies and diamond set in yellow gold.
(Jewellery by Graff)

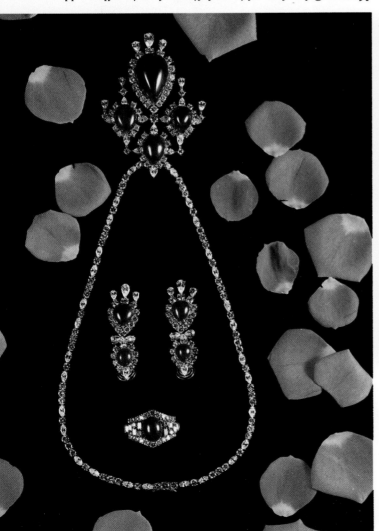

of a garnet.

Of course, there is the long-held belief that gemstones ward off sickness, and this was very much in evidence during the Middle Ages. For example, it was thought that garnets were a remedy for a feverish illness. The Zircon was popular in the 14th century as a safeguard against the Black Death and diamonds were also thought to be a protection against plague.

At this time the opal was known as opthalmioe, or eye-stone. When wrapped in a bayleaf and worn constantly it was thought to improve the eyesight. The emerald has had a connection with eyes for centuries past. This could be considered as part of the reason why green is supposed to be the most restful colour for the eyes. Going back to Roman times, Nero, who had very bad vision, was said to use a slice of emerald to improve his sight while watching the gladiators in the arena.

The idea that gemstones relieved poisons is reflected in the belief that if an emerald was worn when someone had been given poison, that person would immediately break into a sweat which cleared the system. It was also thought that swallowing a draught of powdered agate cured snakebite.

Illness has always been a preoccupation of many people. Further beliefs in the medicinal power of gemstones include the ruby as relieving pain and curing rheumatism. The agate was supposed to be an aid for lung troubles and if an amethyst was worn it would ward off drunkenness. The sapphire when powdered and actually taken in milk was thought to alleviate hysteria. For prevention against asthma and insomnia, powdered topaz was a recommended remedy.

In Medieval times people thought that gemstones lost their brilliance when ill-fortune was forecast and only regained their lustre when the future looked brighter; amazingly this mistaken idea persists today. The theory that gemstones change colour is completely unfounded and must be regarded as a misconception. If there is a variation in colour the difference is caused by certain factors including varying lights because of weather conditions, the time of day or shadow due to artificial light. Experts agree that this fallacy of colour change in

Below: *Ruby and diamond bracelet with matching earrings, pearl and diamond necklace, emerald and diamond bracelet. (Philip Antrobus Ltd.)*

Overleaf: *Left: 9 ct. gold and tortoiseshell pendant. Centre: 9 ct. gold and Mexican lace agate pendant. Right: 9 ct. gold and jasper heart pendant. (Booty Jewellery)*

gemstones must be exposed as nothing more than an old wives' tale.

The subject of superstitions and legends is time-absorbing. The following are chosen at random and pose fascinating assumptions. One of them, dating back to ancient times, alleged that sardonyx was of special benefit to orators, lawyers and bashful suitors. A story is told of a penniless young lawyer who could only afford to rent a ring of red and white banded sardonyx to wear at the hearing of his first case. After some stormy proceedings the power of the sardonyx was so great that the young man won the trial, acquired success and presumably could buy his own sardonyx. During the 17th century, most gentlemen of quality

wore a turquoise ring as it was believed that in the case of a fall from a horse or some height, the turquoise would absorb the force of the impact, so that the owner would not suffer any broken bones. Amber was sometimes called sunstone and was thought to be the hardened tears of the weeping daughters of the sun-god, Apollo.

A final superstition found in ancient lore encompasses all gemstones, maintaining that in order to bring good luck a gemstone must be given freely, never coveted and never taken by fraud or force.

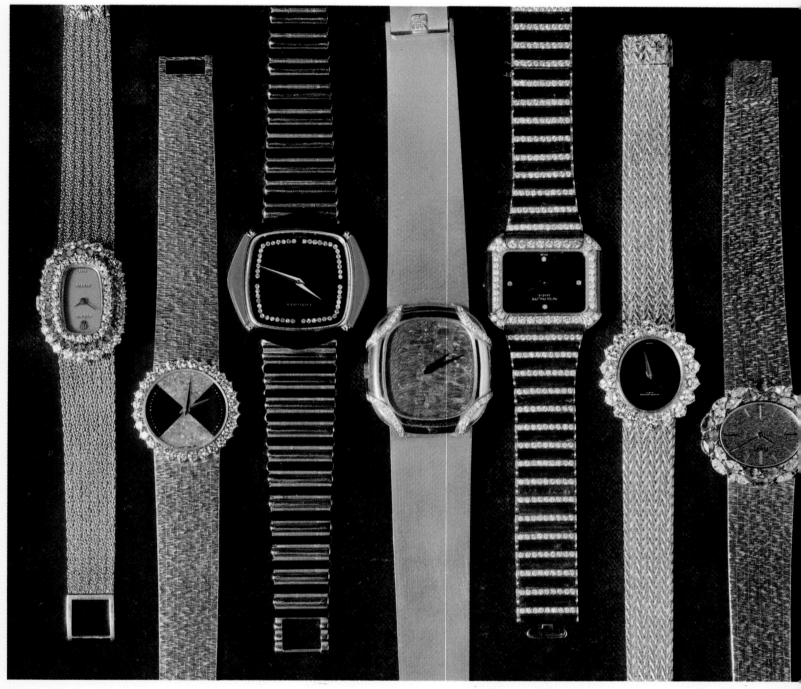

6. The Watch as a Jewel

The craft of watch-making had a long association with Nuremberg, covering almost two centuries since the first stirrings of the industry occurred there around 1500. It was then that Nuremberg was the European craft centre, where, as well as watch-making and an early form of diamond cutting, locksmithing was the main occupation. In fact, records show that the watchmakers were originally locksmiths and the two trades were closely allied.

The invention of the coil spring made possible the introduction of portable clocks and watches. The first portable watch is reputed to have been made before 1500. Indications from the early 16th century suggest that watches could be worn on the breast or, more usually, carried in a purse which hung from a girdle around the waist. The earliest dated watch, presently on show at the Louvre, in Paris, was made by Jacques

Below: *Left to right: 18 ct. white gold bark finished bracelet watch, marquise diamond and emerald bezel. 18 ct. yellow gold woven bracelet watch, upright oval onyx dial with diamond bezel. 18 ct. yellow gold and lapis lazuli, pavé set diamond bracelet watch with quarter set diamond lapis dial. 18 ct. yellow gold bracelet watch fitted opal dial with pavé set diamond corners. 18 ct. yellow gold and onyx link bracelet watch, onyx dial and onyx coral bezel. 18 ct. yellow gold bark finished bracelet round opal and onyx dial with diamond bezel. 18 ct. white gold bracelet watch with triple bezel in diamond and emeralds. (Watches of Switzerland Ltd.)*

Below: *White gold bracelet watch. Mother of Pearl dial with onyx and diamond bezel. (Piaget)*

Above: *Marquise set diamond and ruby watch. Set in a marquise diamond bracelet with rubies. (Piaget)*

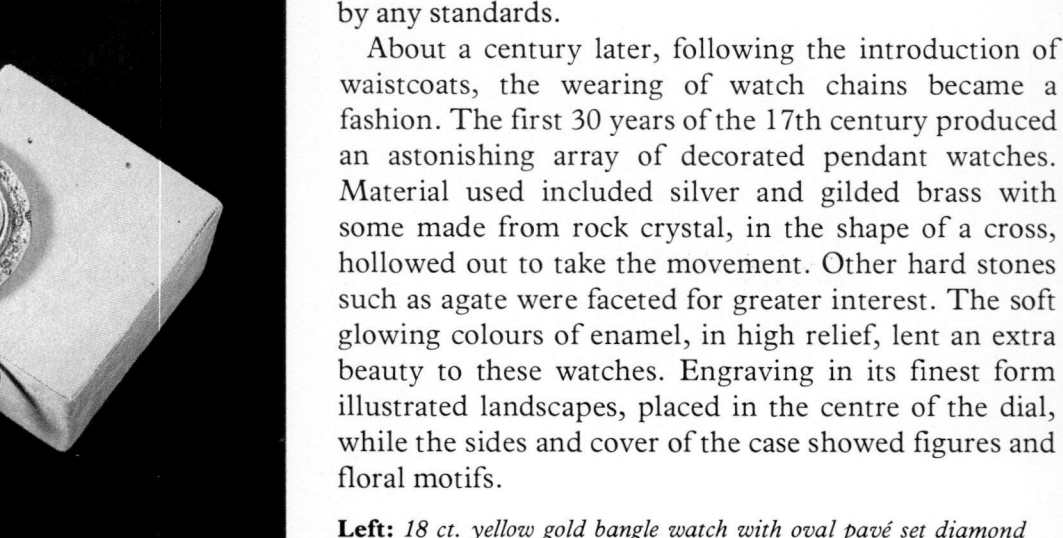

Above: *Left to right: 18 ct. yellow gold and onyx link bracelet watch diamond set onyx dial, and onyx coral bezel. 18 ct. yellow gold bracelet watch fired opal dial with pavé set diamond corners. 18 ct. yellow gold and lapis lazuli and pavé-set diamond bracelet watch with quarter set, diamond lapis dial. (Watches of Switzerland Ltd.)*

de la Garde of Blois, in France, during the year 1551. This portable timepiece is spherical in shape. Another interesting historical note of the 16th century tells that in her will dated 1566, Mary Queen of Scots left Darnley, her second husband and father of James I of England, 'One watch garnished with 10 diamonds, two rubies and a cord of gold': certainly a jewel of a watch, by any standards.

About a century later, following the introduction of waistcoats, the wearing of watch chains became a fashion. The first 30 years of the 17th century produced an astonishing array of decorated pendant watches. Material used included silver and gilded brass with some made from rock crystal, in the shape of a cross, hollowed out to take the movement. Other hard stones such as agate were faceted for greater interest. The soft glowing colours of enamel, in high relief, lent an extra beauty to these watches. Engraving in its finest form illustrated landscapes, placed in the centre of the dial, while the sides and cover of the case showed figures and floral motifs.

Left: *18 ct. yellow gold bangle watch with oval pavé set diamond dial and diamond bezel. (Watches of Switzerland Ltd.)*

During the 18th century, the fantasy watches of the period were quite ingenious. In the Usher Collection there are two remarkable examples. One is in the form of a strawberry; red enamel is picked out in gold to give the effect of the markings on the fruit and the gold stem is curled into a loop for the chain or ribbon to pass through, on which it is hung. The other, an exquisite mandolin in blue enamel, has a delicate central motif in the form of a gold flower, together with a matching fragment of music manuscript; to complete the harmony of design, pearls are inset around the edge. In the same collection a 19th century example, shaped like a beetle, has expanding wings and ruby eyes; the gold case is set with rose diamonds.

The first wrist watch for women appeared about 1900 and was really a compromise. The existing fob watch was attached to a leather strap and then worn around the wrist. After the 1914-1918 war, plain cases and styles gave way to more exotic designs, in keeping with

Left: *Marquise set diamonds and sapphire bracelet with a pavé set diamond dial. (Piaget)*

Below Left: *Sapphire and diamond clasp quartz bracelet watch with pavé set diamond dial and diamond bezel. (Piaget)*

Below Right: *Emerald and diamond bracelet and bezel. (Piaget)*

Overleaf: *Sapphire and diamond trellis watch bracelet, white gold and ruby watch, white gold and onyx watch, yellow gold and diamond pocket watch. (Jewellery by Graff)*

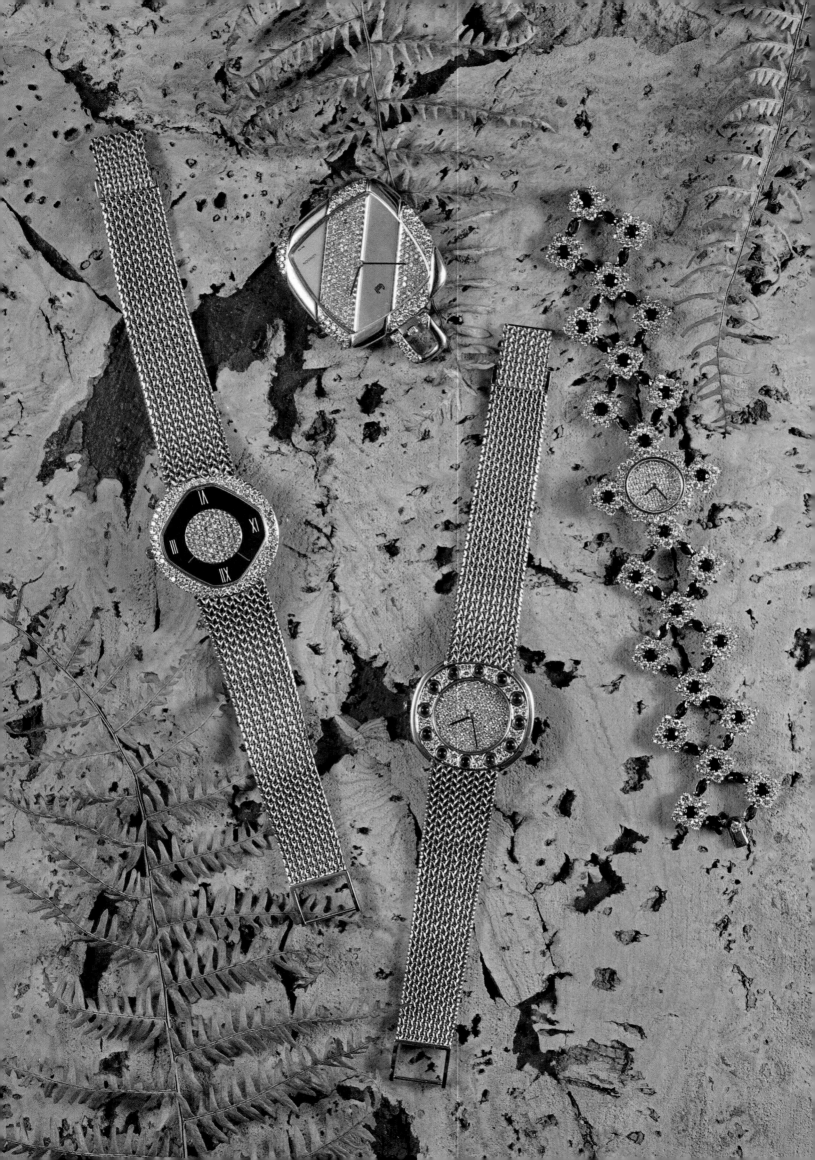

the jewellery of the time. The quiet revolution in watch design happened in the Sixties and achieved quite startling results. No fanfare sounded and comparatively little acclaim was made, but it happened just the same, with far-reaching results. The practical side of time-keeping and the artistic merit of good design are now merged to produce an adornment that works: in fact, the watch as a jewel.

Probably the most significant change in watch design is the harmonizing of the three major elements: in the case, dial and bracelet. There is a recent trend for the case to appear to crown the bracelet. This is a later version of the design where the inset dial seems to be an integral part of the whole. Colour and value have been brought to dials, like a fragment of a stained glass window, and gemstones are used. Coloured blue, green or pink these are lapis lazuli, malachite and coral. Others include the tawny tiger eye, elegant black onyx and translucent opal. Favourite shapes are the simple circle and the oval, worn either vertically or horizontally. Sometimes the beauty of the gemstones is not disturbed by markings, time being indicated only by the position of the hands. Adding to the total harmony these are usually two shafts of gold, and for an even more luxurious interpretation, diamond-set hands seem to illumine the gemstone dials. There is quite a variation in the contemporary type of gold bracelet and among the most popular is the basket weave with fine mesh, a rich brocade effect and a soft satin finish, all equally fashionable. Where styling is concerned, some are delicately tapered, while others come in broad bands of yellow or white gold to complete the lavish approach of the watch as a jewel.

Diamonds have indeed come to have an influence on watch design. Their unique brilliance emphasises the purity of a gold bracelet, stresses the colour of a particular gemstone dial and adds to the clarity of the watch glass. Pavé-set diamonds lend themselves to dials. The word pavé comes from the French word meaning paved and is an apt description. This style has the diamonds placed so closely together that none of the precious metal in which they are set can be seen. An arresting design quarters the dial into pavé-set diamonds and black onyx, surrounded by brilliant diamonds, with a textured 18-carat white gold bracelet. The surround of a watch is known as the bezel. Derived from the French word biseau, meaning bevel, it is simply the grooved rim of the dial into which the watch glass is set.

Among many exquisite contemporary designs there is one that has a combination of diamonds, emeralds and a black opal. The dial is a black opal with shafts of white gold for hands framed in brilliant cut diamonds on a delicate double banded diamond bracelet. A trail of marquise cut emeralds wreathes around the case to make a watch of sheer perfection. Now that the watch is a jewel, it can be worn with pride, like any other treasured possession.

Top Right: *Diamond and 18 ct. white gold bracelet watch with skeleton movement by Vacheron et Constantin.*
(Garrard The Crown Jewellers)

Left: *18 ct. white gold double bezel in diamonds and emeralds.*
(Watches of Switzerland Ltd.)

Below: 18 ct. white gold bracelet watches. Left to right: Onyx dial, lapis lazuli dial, malachite dial. All with diamond set bezels. (Piaget)

Right: *Mediaeval devotional and talismanic rings. Left: gold Saint Christopher, inscribed inside De bon cor. English: 15th century, 692-1871. Right: gold, inscribed Ave Mar Gracia. English 14th century. Museum number 635-1871. Both Waterton Collection. (Victoria and Albert Museum)*

Below: *Pendant. The Armada (Heneage) Jewel. Enamelled gold pendant set with diamonds and rubies. In front is a portrait bust of Queen Elizabeth and inside is a miniature portrait of the Queen. The back is enamelled with the same device as appears on the Armada Medal. This jewel is said to have been given by the Queen to Sir Thomas Heneage (d.1595) a Privy Councillor and Vice Chamberlain of the Royal Household. English circa 1588. Museum number 81-1935. From the J. Pierpoint Morgan Collection. (Victoria & Albert Museum)*

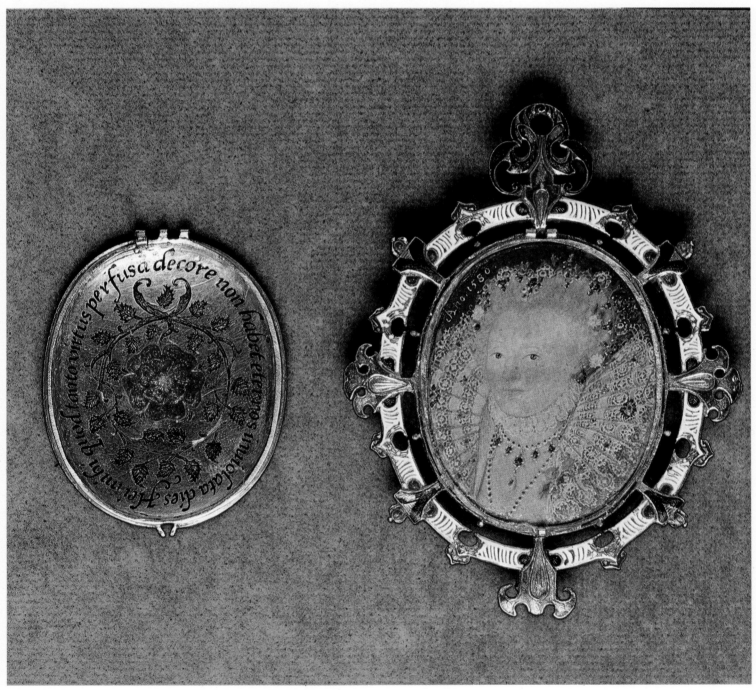

Below: *Pendant. Enamelled gold, set with spinels, crystals, and an emerald, hung with pearls. Spanish (Barcelona), about 1600. Museum number 334-1870. From the treasure of Virgin of the Pillar, Saragossa. (Victoria & Albert Museum)*

The Jewellery Collection at the Victoria & Albert Museum in London is probably the most comprehensive in the world. There may be larger displays or perhaps more impressive individual objects contained in public collections abroad, but this representative collection shows examples from Ancient Egypt right up to the present day. As well as precious jewellery there is a unique range of peasant jewellery from many countries.

The Jewellery Collection is as old as the museum itself. It all began when the Great Exhibition of 1851 closed. The Treasury had authorised a then nominal sum to be spent on buying from the Exhibition such objects of applied art excelling in workmanship, yet without reference to particular styles. Included were examples of contemporary French jewellery, which were put on view at Marlborough House, in London's Pall Mall, during 1852, first known as The Museum of Manufactures. Later in the same year it came to be called The Museum of Ornamental Art and began to collect historical jewellery.

Above: *Pendant. The Armada Jewel. Enamelled gold pendant set with diamonds and rubies. Left: Enamelled plaque on the back of the pendant, showing the Ark, without frame. Right: Front of the pendant showing Queen Elizabeth. Museum number 81-1935. (Victoria & Albert Museum)*

Left: *Pendant. The Armada Jewel. Enamelled gold pendant set with diamonds and rubies. Back cover of the pendant, showing the Ark, within its strapwork frame. Museum number 81-1935. (Victoria & Albert Museum)*

Below: Roman ring. Gold, set with a sardonyx intaglio of Abundantia. Roman, 2nd or 3rd century A.D. Museum number 460-1871. Waterton Collection. (Victoria & Albert Museum)

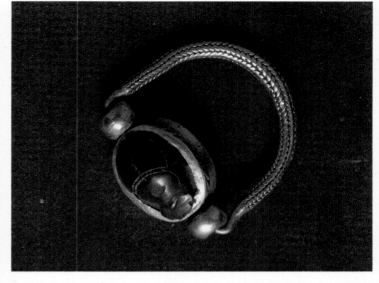

Below: Ancient Egyptian ring in gold. The hoop of close corded work has a revolving bezel, set with a bloodstone scarab engraved with Isis nursing Horus. Phoenician: 6th century BC. Waterton Collection. Museum number 408-1871. (Victoria & Albert Museum)

Above: Gorget, gold, repoussé. Irish circa 7th century B.C. Found near Shannongrove, County Limerick, in the mid-18th century, and formerly an heirloom of the Earls of Charleville. Given by Colonel C.K. Howard Bury, D.S.O. Museum number 35-1948. (Victoria & Albert Museum)

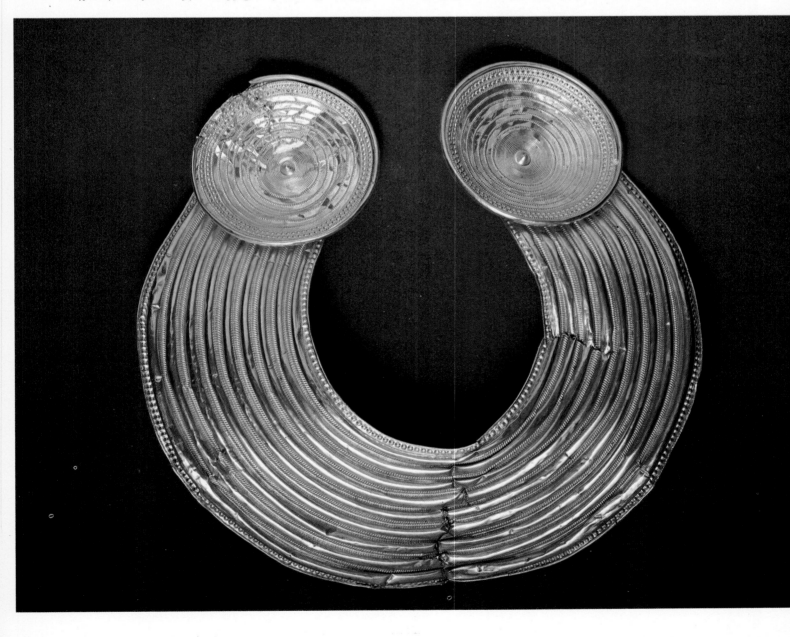

When Marlborough House was needed as a residence for the then Prince of Wales, later King Edward VII, other accommodation had to be found. The Museum moved to its present site in the South Kensington area of London and came to be called The Museum of Science and Art. The year was 1857 and by this time the historic specimens of jewellery outnumbered the modern ones.

In 1891 a design was needed for the rebuilding of certain parts of the Museum; a competition took place and it was won by Aston Webb who subsequently was knighted. Nine years went by before the foundation stone was laid in 1899, which was also the last public ceremony attended by Queen Victoria, and it was then that she made the request for the Museum to be called the Victoria & Albert Museum.

Below: *Gem: Pale bluish-grey star sapphire showing six rayed star. From the Rev. Chauncey Hare Townshend Bequest made in 1869. Museum number 1245-1869. (Victoria & Albert Museum)*

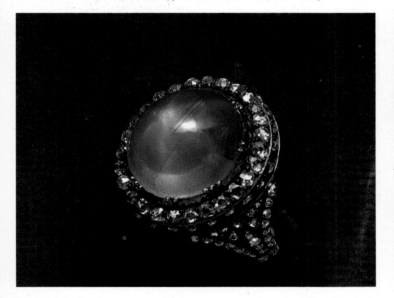

Below: *Left: Gem — mixed cut peridot in ring. Museum number 1302-1869.*
Right: Gems — pale amethyst with smoky quartz. Museum number 1186-1869.
Both are from the Rev. Chauncey Hare Townshend Bequest made in 1869. (Victoria & Albert Museum)

Above: *Gem: An interesting scalloped gold setting for the large blue oval aquamarine. From the Rev. Chauncey Hare Townshend Bequest made in 1869. Museum number 1288-1869. (Victoria & Albert Museum)*

Eight years afterwards, in June 1909, the present building was opened by King Edward VII, with great pomp, it having cost one million pounds. This highly ornamented edifice with terra cotta decoration has a crowning cupola that looks like the tiers of some grand wedding cake, presided over by the figure of Fame. The treasures it houses include the fine and applied arts of all countries, periods and styles and is unrivalled for its quality and scope.

Although jewellery pieces had continued to be bought from International Exhibitions, up to the Paris Exhibition of 1900, it is interesting to note that the Jewellery Collection has been mainly built up from gifts. One notable bequest is the Waterton Collection of rings. There are examples of Ancient Egyptian scarabs, Roman intaglios, a type of cameo of the 1st century A.D, medieval Devotional and Talismanic rings of the 13th and 18th centuries: in fact a most remarkable historical survey of rings.

Another interesting exhibit is the outstanding group of gemstones mounted as rings. These were bequeathed to the Museum in 1869 by the Rev. Chauncey Hare Townshend, and there are 183 of these fascinating stones. Of particular note are the aquamarine, the peridot and the deep purple amethyst. Star rubies and sapphires have a special interest but once again it is the variety and breadth of this collection that has most appeal.

Among the best known European pieces on show is an Irish collar of the 7th century B.C. in the form of a magnificent gold torque. From the 16th century there is the Armada jewel; in blue enamelled gold it is set with diamonds and rubies. On the front of the case there is a portrait bust of Queen Elizabeth I and inside is a tiny miniature portrait of the Queen, possibly by Nicholas Hilliard and later retouched. From the Cathedral treasury of the Virgin of the Pillar, Saragossa, in Spain, a pendant of enamelled gold hung with pearls, is set with spinels, crystals and an emerald. In the centre is a dog, a favourite motif of that time, about 1600. Dress ornaments from the Russian Crown Jewels of the late 18th century include a gold and silver flower brooch, decorated with enamelling and heavily encrusted with diamonds and rubies.

Facing Page: *Spray Ornament. Gold and silver, enamelled and set with rubies and diamonds. Once a bodice ornament mounted on a pin, later converted into a brooch. Russian, about 1780, from the Russian Crown Jewels. Museum number 85-1951. Cory Bequest. (Victoria and Albert Museum)*

Below: *Gem: Large blue oval aquamarine, a member of the beryl family. From the Rev. Chauncey Hare Townshend Bequest made in 1869. Museum number 1288-1869. (Victoria & Albert Museum)*

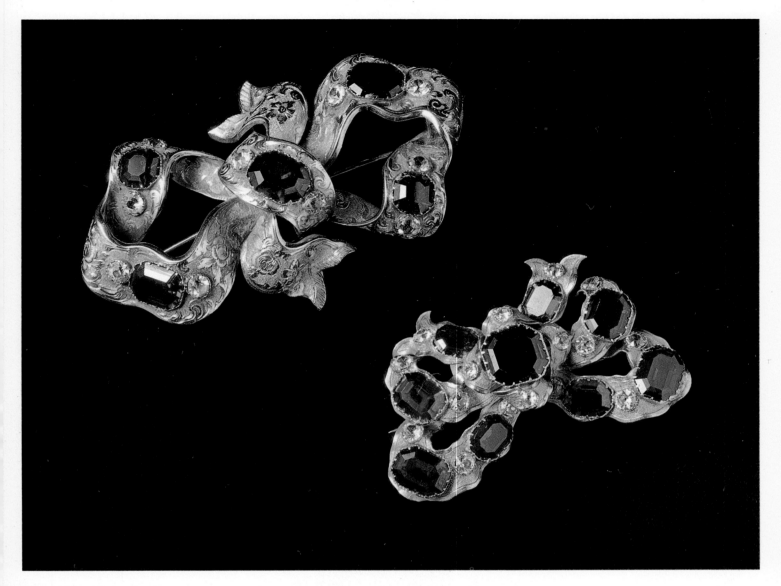

8. Some Design Trends in Jewellery from the 18th, 19th and 20th Centuries

Trends in jewellery design are a fascinating study. They recall an entire period and recapture much of the atmosphere of the time. The Georgian period was essentially feminine. Much of the jewellery set out to flatter slender necks, complement well-formed ears and emphasise shapely hands. Ingenuity played its part in the make-up of the pieces.

An example of this inventiveness can be seen in the 'tremblant' or trembling effect applied to the brooch and hair ornament. Movement was achieved by attaching the jewel, on a fine spiral spring, to its pin or clasp. The diamonds shimmered and caught the light, even when the wearer was sitting still. Quiet breathing

Right: Georgian 18 ct. yellow gold filigree cross pendant set with garnets and half pearls on a gold link belcher chain. (Richard Ogden Ltd.)

Below: Larger bow: chrysolite and garnet in 18 ct. gold bow brooch with flower design engraved in relief. Smaller bow: chrysolite and garnet bow brooch set in 18 ct. gold. (Richard Ogden Ltd.)

Above: *A suite of five Georgian diamond stars mounted in silver and gold. Can be worn as a tiara, brooches or hair piece decorations. (Garrard The Crown Jewellers)*

Below: *Georgian collet necklace set with topaz coloured French paste and set in gold, Georgian oval topaz ring surrounded by half pearls. All set in gold with seed pearl set "Fleur de Lys" shoulders, cushion shaped topaz and diamond cluster ring in gold. (Richard Ogden Ltd)*

was enough to activate the springs.

The practical aspect of Georgian society is summed up in the way diamond jewellery was created as a whole but could be separated into sections, to form different pieces. Flowers were very popular in design and large blooms could be taken apart to become a set of brooches with matching earrings. A spray brooch could be formed by fastening the leaves together and smaller leaves could be linked to the scrolled stalks to make a necklace and matching bracelet.

Magnificent diamond pendant earrings were much in evidence and reflected the design of the huge chandeliers, necessary to light the ballrooms of this particular period. Diamonds were also used in the tiaras, or fenders, as they were called in Georgian times. Leaves, flowers and ears of wheat were other design favourites.

Brooches were mainly in the form of the marguerite or the rose. One lovely example of a rose has topaz petals, emerald leaves and ruby-set buds, but diamond bows and feathers were also popular. At the beginning of the 18th century designs were rather formal and representational, but towards its end a more naturalistic style developed so that the flowers looked as if they might be real, with a textured stem and even a tiny dragonfly or butterfly hovering above them.

Long strings of matching pearls were also fashionable, not always worn simply around the neck, but on occasions knotted on the shoulder and casually worn across the body. Chokers rarely encircled the neck completely and were secured at the nape by a bow of velvet ribbon: a flattering way with neckwear for the

Above: *Georgian garnet coloured French paste collet necklace set in gold. Georgian almandine garnet and silver spray brooch. (Richard Ogden Ltd.)*

Facing Page: *Georgian set, consisting pink topaz and gold necklace, earrings, brooch and pendant, circa 1800. (Philip Antrobus Ltd.)*

Below: *An oval pavé set cushion-shaped diamond ring, with red enamel surround, circa 1800. A George III openwork diamond ring of cross design set with cushion and pear-shaped diamonds closed gold back, circa 1780. (Bonhams Auctioneers)*

very young with swan-like necks.

Gold chatelaines were widely worn hooked to the dress. From these decorated plaques hung chains from which were suspended such objects as a seal, a watch, a key, a writing tablet and even a miniature sewing set. Essentially practical, this type of jewel was worn only during the day.

Rings were a favourite form of jewellery, a characteristic design of the time being the single stone or cluster in a cupped setting, the shank and shoulders deeply chiselled with scrolls. Anticipating the eternity ring of the present day, diamonds were set round a simple hoop and emphasised the elegant white hand of the 18th century Court Lady. After 1760 there was an innovation in ring design. This was the 'marquise', shaped like an oval with pointed ends. It could have one coloured stone, probably a ruby or sapphire, surrounded by diamonds or have an enamel background

Facing Page: *An early 19th century foiled pink topaz and gold filigree work cruciform pendant. English. (Cameo Corner Ltd.)*

Left: *An enamelled gold portrait ring, set with diamonds. English, 18th century. (Cameo Corner Ltd.)*

Below: *Antique diamond lozenge brooch in silver and gold circa 1821. Antique diamond bow brooch with pavé set diamond detachable heart mounted in silver and gold, circa 1870. (Garrard The Crown Jewellers)*

possibly set with a single diamond or pearl.

Diamonds were undoubtedly the favourite precious stone of the Georgian period but other gems used in ornamental motifs included the topaz, the amethyst, the garnet, the opal and the peridot.

Towards the close of the 18th century Wedgwood cameos were an important contribution to new jewellery styles of the era. Of hard paste, made from black basalt and jasper, the subjects were mainly classical scenes on Greco-Roman lines.

The Victorian period saw a bewildering array of design in jewellery, partly due to the Industrial Revolution and the increased prosperity of certain stratas of society. During the early part, the designs were delicate and imaginative, borrowing from the

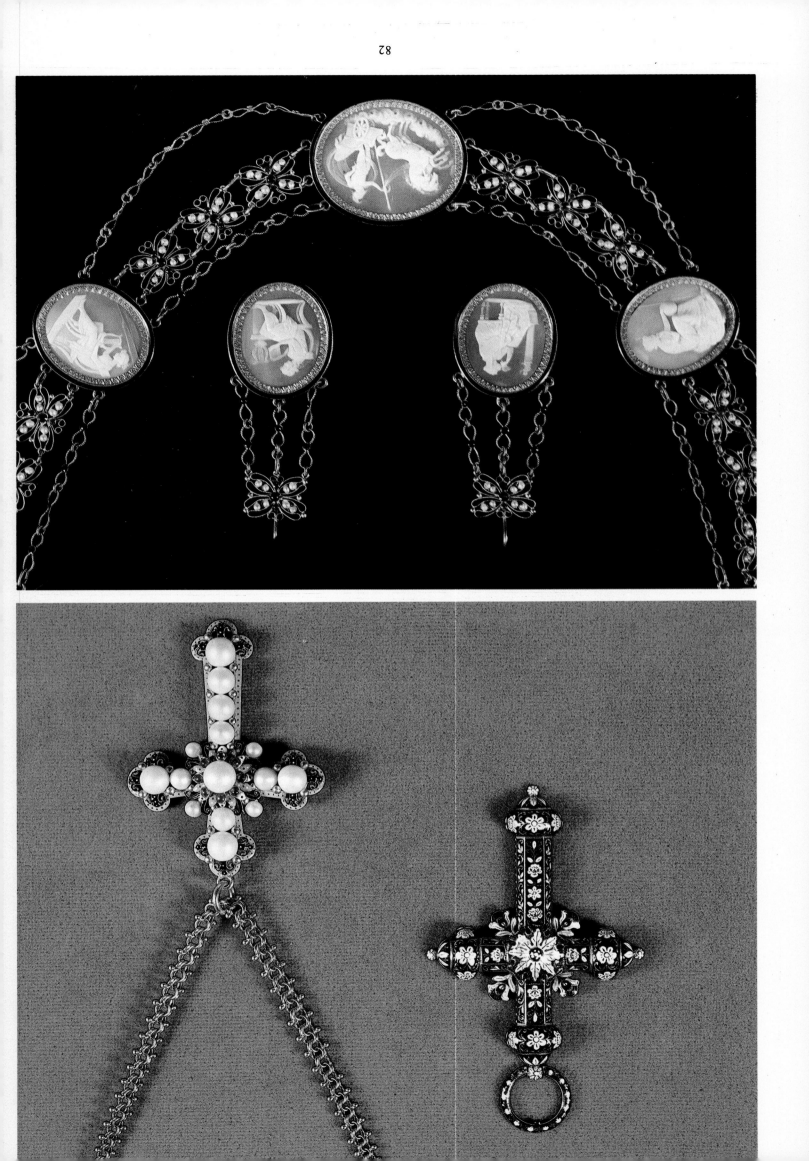

but reached its peak of popularity after the death of the Prince Consort in 1861, when mourning became more overt. This was the time for 'memento mori'; a lock of the departed's hair was encased in a brooch, under glass, for all to see, or intricately woven to form a pattern for a brooch.

The mid-Victorians were besotted with designs in gold representing birds, bees, butterflies and dragonflies, all set with gemstones of the period. Even the unlovely house-fly was enshrined as a brooch. The wings glittered with rose diamonds and the body was set with green peridots.

Garnet rings, in a dome shape, with a golden star or tiny seed pearls inset, were very much of the period. Turquoise and coral were two favourite gemstones. Small girls wore coral earrings and necklaces in an attempt to copy their older sisters in the large families of that time.

From 1885 to 1901 there was a return to the more delicate approach to jewellery. It was worn discreetly and diamonds again came to the fore. Other gems were

Renaissance, the Middle Ages and the natural world. Seed pearls were woven in and out of demure hair styles and later combined with various gemstones such as amethyst, garnet, cornelian and opal — to form rings, brooches, bracelets and earrings. The serpent theme, dating back to Roman times, was popular; indeed Queen Victoria's bethrothal ring was of that design. Gold tassel jewellery was favoured around the 1840's; this arose from the Algerian Wars then raging, when the soldiers' uniforms were embellished with this type of decoration and so gold tassels were adopted as a fashion note.

After 1860 Victorian taste was much occupied with Gothic architecture and this was reflected in the jewellery, massive gold pieces of geometric precision being popular. Queen Victoria's passion for Balmoral Castle led to the popularity of grouse claws and dirks as brooches, set with amethysts and cairngorms. Whitby jet was carved and used in jewellery from about 1800,

Right: *A Limoges enamel of a young lady in Renaissance costume, set in a border of pearls and gold. French, circa 1870. (Hancocks & Co. Ltd.)*

Facing Page, Top: *A fine enamelled gold, ruby and pearl trefoil cross, the arms of flecked powder blue enamel set with freshwater pearls, with a similarly decorated cabochon ruby flowerhead motif at the centre 3″ high, circa 1880. (Asprey & Co. Ltd.)*

Left: *A gold mounted shell cameo, enamel and seed pearl necklace with matching earrings, the cameos carved with classical subjects. French early 19th century. (Cameo Corner Ltd.)*

muted to offset the diamond brilliance and included pearls, opals and moonstones. These last were considered lucky and sometimes were carved into cherubs, hearts, crescents and suns.

During the reign of Edward VII, imposing diamond jewellery set in gold was much in evidence. A long, narrow diamond necklace supported, for example, an impressive cross, pendant or tassel, also set with diamonds. Magnificent tiaras were taller, so that the diamonds caught the light, while enormous shoulder knots and floral sprays were the perfect setting for the larger diamonds.

Owing to technical advancements in the working of platinum, this precious metal began to be used widely. Because of its strength it could be used in particularly fine and delicate designs, and a lattice effect was among the most popular. Platinum was not hallmarked until the Hallmarking Act of 1973, implemented in 1975, when it took its place alongside the other precious metals.

Few significant innovations were made during the years 1914 to 1918, with one notable exception, the introduction of white gold. Experiments had been made, covering many years, but it became a commercial possibility during the war years when money was scarce.

Top Right: *An opal matrix brooch of Mendaus. Italian — late 19th century. (Hancocks & Co. Ltd.)*

Above: *A gold mounted bangle set with rubies, pearls and diamonds and decorated with white champlevé enamel, the centrepiece being removed to wear as a pendant. English, mid-19th century. (Cameo Corner Ltd.)*

Left: *Ruby, sapphire and brilliant cut diamond bee. Circa 1870. (Garrard The Crown Jewellers)*

Facing Page: *A group of 19th century sardonyx and onyx cameo brooches in decorative gold, pearl and enamel frames of French, English and Italian origins. (Cameo Corner Ltd.)*

Above: A Victorian diamond "Wild Rose" spray mounted in silver and gold. English, circa 1860. (Hancocks & Co. Ltd.)

(Bonham's Auctioneers)

Below: A Victorian gold strawberry red guilloche enamel brooch with split pearl flower spray centre, circa 1860-70.

Above: An early Victorian blue enamel, pearl, rose diamond and gold scroll and leaf design bangle. (Cameo Corner Ltd.)

Previous page: *An important amethyst, chased and embossed gold necklace and earrings, the centrepiece of the necklace detaching for use as a brooch. English, mid-Victorian. (Cameo Corner Ltd.)*

Below: *An embossed gold bracelet set with a Roman mosaic. English and Italian, mid-Victorian. (Cameo Corner Ltd.)*

Above: *Victorian ruby emerald and diamond butterfly brooch with an opal body mounted "en tremblant". (Asprey & Co. Ltd.)*

Below: *A Victorian gold, baroque pearl, diamond and rust coloured enamel flower spray brooch. Circa 1850-60. (Bonhams Auctioneers)*

and platinum too costly. It is interesting to note that gold when mined is yellow. The colour however can be varied by the addition of various metals, to produce the required carat content and appropriate colour. With white gold the proportion of silver or palladium is increased and in the case of red gold there is more copper added.

With the twenties there emerged a whole new movement which influenced architecture, furniture, dress and, of course, jewellery. The standard of craftmanship was quite exceptional, with the emphasis on precision. Jewellery designs were flat and markedly severe. The geometric shapes had a cut-out background, with the spaces playing their part in the over-all concept. To demonstrate the careful workmanship, in some cases gems such as sapphires

Below: *An important Art Nouveau plique á jour enamel and gold locket set with rubies and rose diamonds. French, circa 1895. (Hancocks & Co. Ltd.)*

Left: *A dragonfly with "plique á jour" enamel wings (giving a stained glass window effect), a diamond tail and an enamelled gold and rose diamond head. French, circa 1910. (Hancocks & Co. Ltd.)*

Below: *An important Art Deco calibre sapphire and diamond pierced circle in a millegrain platinum mount. French, circa 1930. (Hancocks & Co. Ltd.)*

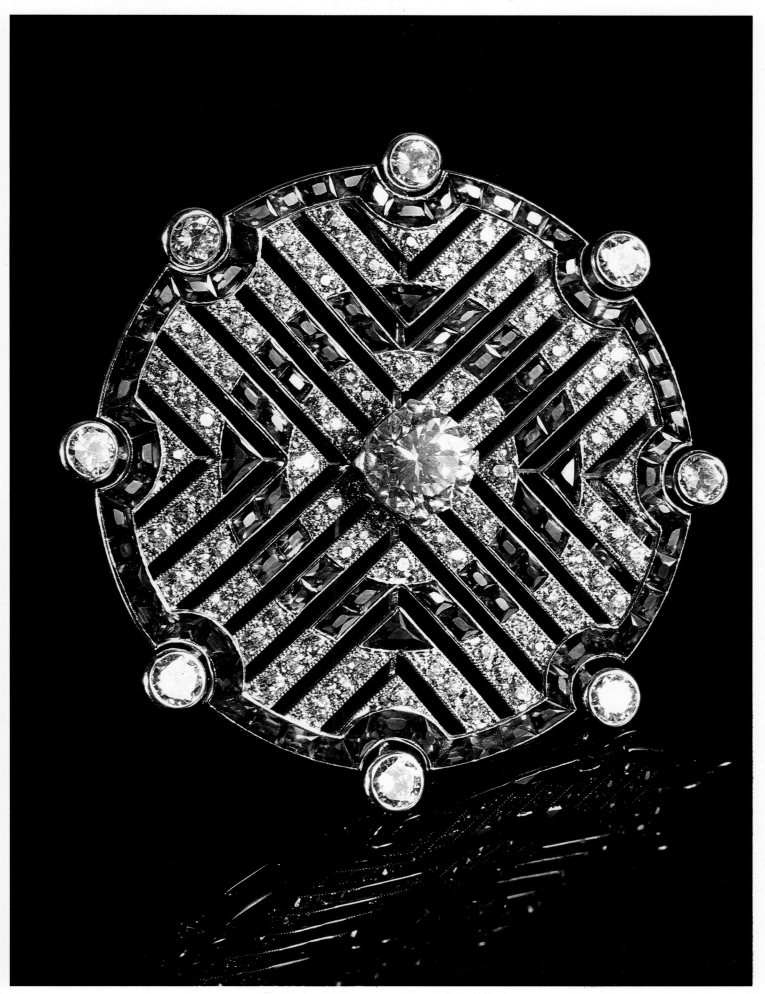

Above: *Diamond butterfly brooch with antique turquoise and gold snake bracelet. (Philip Antrobus Ltd.)*

Right: *Art Deco jade, cabochon ruby and diamond single clip. American, circa 1935. (Hancocks & Co. Ltd.)*

and rubies were specially cut to fit into the open parts of the pattern.

Until the fifties there was a return to the more three-dimensional approach, with rather florid scroll or floral designs, usually of diamonds. A fashion note of the time was the single dress clip of diamonds, but occasionally using emeralds, sapphires and rubies. This particular feature developed into a double dress clip. Worn together as brooch, or singly as clips on either side of a neckline, these elaborate jewelled accessories were again mainly of diamonds. Two-coloured golds made their appearance and also gave depth to designs. Featured in brooches, red and yellow golds were either highly burnished or had a matt finish. For added decoration, rubies were chosen to offset the rich qualities of the precious metal.

The early fifties saw some interesting fashion ideas for jewellery. In haute couture precious stones were used as buttons, even on fine tweed dresses. Focus was placed on the fashionable nipped-in waistline with jewelled belts sewn with seed pearls, turquoise and crystal beads. Chokers were featured widely; they could be of gold, three of four rows of pearls or even a broad

Left: *Diamond and emerald ring, opal and diamond ring. (Philip Antrobus Ltd.)*

Below: *A platinum and diamond set "Prowling Fox" with ruby eyes and enamel fangs. English circa 1920. (Hancocks & Co. Ltd.)*

band of precious stones. Long pendant earrings were also popular. An upsurge of interest in pierced ears made it possible to wear the fashionable, heavier type earrings. Brooches became more versatile and were used with ingenuity to decorate hats, lapels and waists.

Towards the end of the sixties the natural gem crystal, uncut by the lapidary, became extremely popular. Used in rings and organic-type pendants, the gold or silver settings were claw-like and minimal. A selection of agate, amethyst, citrine, tourmaline and malachite was among the gems that showed varying degrees of the same colour, to make an arresting piece of jewellery.

As the seventies progressed, settings began to become an integral part of the whole design. In order to promote a proper harmony, precious metals and gemstones were equally balanced. Another interesting change was the way that extravagant jewellery fashions of the late sixties and early seventies gave way to a more restrained and wearable approach to design, better suited to the strains and pressures of the time.

As is traditional, jewellery design, today, exploits the prevailing technical abilities within the craft, so that art and the practical approach are inextricably combined to produce an adornment that is a visual delight.

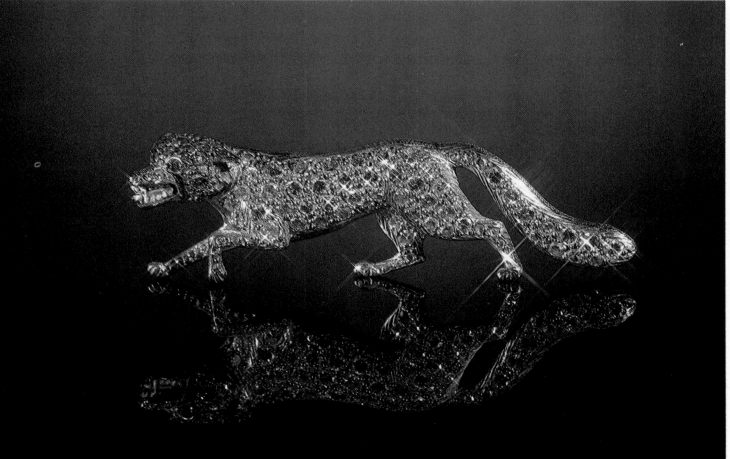

Below: *Yellow gold, emerald and diamond necklace with two heart-shaped emeralds and navette diamond clusters. (Cartier, London)*